PRAISE FOR *GARDENTOPIA*

"*Gardentopia* is that rare marriage of the *art* of landscaping and the technical *knowledge* of how to compose a landscape—boiled down to readily understood and easily executed actions. This book puts you in the driver's seat and shows you how to chart the course to your own personal garden utopia."

—Margie Grace, APLD International Landscape Designer of the Year, Grace Design Associates

"The topic of garden design has been covered in a myriad of ways, but Jan has put an imaginative new spin on it. Years of landscape design experience paired with beautiful attention to detail evolve into this lovely new approach. I was excited to turn every page in order to explore Jan's next take on artful accents, paths, themes, color, and plants. *Gardentopia* will become an essential source for my design classes, as well as a wealth of inspiration for my own landscape plans."

—Lisa Orgler, PLA, Iowa State University, www.papergardenworkshop.com

"*Gardentopia* is a feast for the eyes and the brain. Jan Johnsen has taken design concepts and made them easy to understand and use in one's own garden. Then, she has supplemented her ideas with beautiful and illustrative photographs. I can hardly wait to implement some of these ideas. This book is destined for my library."

—Bobbie Schwartz, FAPLD

"The design know-how that I've gained through decades of practice is simply laid out here by Jan Johnsen for anyone to understand. From new homeowner to experienced garden designer, this book will take your efforts to a higher level."

—Carl Molter, Landscape Designer, Host/Producer of WDVR FM's *Into the Garden*

"Intriguing to the mindscape, *Gardentopia* offers insightful vistas of inspiration to the gardener in all of us. With respect and gratitude for the years of inspiration and generosity in spirit, thanks to Jan for creating a book that is destined to become a good old friend."

—Michelle Derviss, Michelle Derviss Landscape Design

"Jan Johnsen is one of the most popular writers on GardenDesign.com. Her insights have educated thousands. Her passion has inspired just as many. Now you'll be able to find her insights and the passion in one place."

—Jim Peterson, Publisher, *Garden Design*

GARDENTOPIA

GARDENTOPIA

DESIGN BASICS FOR CREATING BEAUTIFUL OUTDOOR SPACES

Jan Johnsen

THE COUNTRYMAN PRESS
A division of W. W. Norton & Company
Independent Publishers Since 1923

For information about permission to reproduce selections from this book, write to
Permissions, The Countryman Press, 500 Fifth Avenue, New York, NY 10110

For information about special discounts for bulk purchases, please contact
W. W. Norton Special Sales at specialsales@wwnorton.com or 800-233-4830

Manufacturing by Versa Press
Book design by Anna Reich
Production manager: Devon Zahn

The Countryman Press
www.countrymanpress.com

A division of W. W. Norton & Company, Inc.
500 Fifth Avenue, New York, NY 10110
www.wwnorton.com

978-1-68268-396-5

10 9 8 7 6 5 4 3 2

CONTENTS

2. WALLS, PATIOS, WALKS, AND STEPS   90

3. THEME GARDENS   123

INTRODUCTION

*Gradually and silently the charm comes over us; we know not
exactly where or how . . .* —Frederick Law Olmsted

Garden lovers revel in being in an outdoor space filled with flowers,
trees, and artful accents used in imaginative ways. Here, we feel a sense
of well-being that is hard to match. So how can you transform your backyard into a place where, as the great nineteenth-century park designer
Frederick Law Olmsted described, charm descends upon you? This book
outlines the simple changes you can make that will turn your backyard
into what I call a "gardentopia," an outdoor space of delight and serenity.

I have spent my 40-plus years as a professional landscape designer
transforming tough sites into appealing landscapes. I have learned a
lot along the way and I want to share that knowledge with you. *Gardentopia: Design Basics for Creating Beautiful Outdoor Spaces* describes garden-
making techniques that I have found to be especially helpful. Each of the
illustrated suggestions describes a design idea, gardening pointer, or
selected plant that you can use to improve your landscape, no matter its
size. I chose to write it as a series of basic tips so that you can easily grasp
each concept and say, "That's a good idea—I can do that!"

I have always been in the business of creating beautiful landscapes
for others. I studied landscape architecture decades ago, but much of
my design expertise comes from my time working in Japan and Hawaii
when I was a young adult. After returning home to the United States, I
went to work for a Versailles-trained French gardener at a hotel called
the Mohonk Mountain House in New York. It was there that I learned
many of the on-the-ground horticultural techniques I write about. Most
of the photos in this book are landscapes that I created with my firm,
Johnsen Landscapes & Pools, based in Westchester County, New York.
My husband, Rafael Algarin, and I have been running our company for
over 32 years.

Although the landscapes shown in this book are primarily located
in the northeastern United States, the garden tips I describe can be
applied anywhere. Additionally, the captions that accompany some of

the photographs include the story behind the image or describe some interesting detail.

The suggestions in *Gardentopia* are not complicated and span many aspects of landscape design, from configuring an outdoor space to choosing a theme for your garden to selecting the perfect plant. I have focused on these aspects of garden design because I believe that a basic understanding of them can improve both the looks of your garden and the value of your property. And, most of all, these improvements help make your garden a vibrant place where you want to spend time.

For ease of use, I have divided the book into five sections:

1. *Garden Design and Artful Accent Tips*

Site design is the framework that every garden needs. This first section encourages you to look at your yard's layout with fresh eyes. Why not move that hedge, widen a walk, or add a bench? These tips offer ideas on layout, alignment, and more. I also discuss fun additions such as gates, features, and outdoor seating that make a garden distinctly yours.

2. *Walls, Patios, Walks, and Steps*

Hardscape elements such as walks and walls make up the "bones" of an outdoor space. This section gives you tips for the permanent part of a landscape. It offers ideas regarding paving, location of walkways, details such as edging, and other elements. These features are hard to change, once installed, and so you should consider them first before thinking about plants and planting.

3. *Theme Gardens*

Gardens with a singular focus grab the imagination and let us get creative with one fun idea. This section describes special-interest gardens such as a butterfly garden, medicinal garden, tropical garden, and others. We all love themes; they make a garden extra special. This section provides juicy inspiration for such an endeavor.

4. *Color in the Garden*

We see color before anything else in a garden, and the effect it has upon us is fascinating. Here, I celebrate the potency of color and its impact in

Gardenia bushes are warm-weather plants but you can grow it in a pot outdoors in summer. They are prolific bloomers with numerous pointed buds shaped like sea-shells that unfurl to reveal luscious, fragrant white flowers.

an outdoor space. There are so many ways to combine colors, subtly or boldly, in a garden. Once you start down this colorful path, it's hard to turn back. I share ways to use color imaginatively outdoors.

5. *Plants and Planting*

Finally, I touch on everyone's favorite part of a garden: the plants. I describe a few of my favorite go-to plants. This is not a complete list in any way, and I've limited my suggestions to some easy-to-grow and easy-to-appreciate plants. I also offer a few ideas on gardening and maintenance techniques that I have found helpful.

Frederick Law Olmsted said it best when he said that charm comes over us gradually in a garden. That is so true. Here we can relax and delight in the magic of nature's workings. I wish you luck in your garden-making endeavors. And I hope you create a gardentopia of your own.

1.

GARDEN DESIGN *and* ARTFUL ACCENTS

The world is moving into a phase when landscape design may well be recognized as the most comprehensive of the arts.

—Geoffrey Jellicoe

Make a curved flowerbed. The eye-catching sweep of the curve creates an embracing gesture that people love. A low boxwood hedge reinforces the line.

A garden is nature—bounded, protected, and shaped—by our hand. Its form can range from a simple balcony filled with planters to a sweeping vista dotted with trees. No matter which type of garden you have, its layout determines how you experience it. From how you enter the space, to where you sit, to the views offered up, each area must fit snugly within the whole. But how do you do that? How do you arrange your landscape so all areas connect? And how do you incorporate notions of movement and mystery as well? The garden design tips offered here help you do just that. For example, you can create a simple curved plant bed to lead the eye, or you can strategically place a tree to frame a view. If you like design and arranging space, this first section is for you.

Geoffrey Jellicoe, the great English garden writer, designer, and historian, sagely noted that landscape design is "the most comprehensive of the arts." How true that is. We must consider the site, the weather, the layout, the plants, and of course, maintenance. It is quite a complex undertaking if you stop and think about it. But the design of your garden is what comes first, and so I start this book of suggestions with pointers on garden design and decorative accents.

The design ideas I share are a blend of large concepts and small details. Some address the big picture, such as formulating your goal, while others talk about what to do with details like the corners of an outdoor space. These ideas can be used individually or you can implement several tips together. Each adds to the creation of a compelling outdoor space.

I also include tips on garden features in this section. This is the fun part of garden design, and these features refer to anything that adds a personal touch such as a bench, birdbath, sculpture, and more. An artful accent attracts our attention with its color, form, and placement. It greatly affects the space around it. This was observed by the Japanese American designer, Isamu Noguchi:

> An empty space has no visual dimension or significance. Scale and
> meaning enter when some thoughtful object or line is introduced.
> This is why sculptures, or sculptural objects, create space.

Garden design is all about modifying outdoor space to create, as Noguchi says, "scale and meaning." The design tips offered here will help you make your garden a place you love to be in.

Winter and Summer—hard to imagine summer's glory in winter! Here I placed a solitary bench by the water's edge. I added a rock border at the base of a hill with yellow daylilies (Hemerocallis) *dressing up the slope.*

Before and After—imagine how a wall and border can change it all. A new low wall between parking area and terrace creates a safer and more defined layout. The curved steps and Belgian block curbing highlight the transition between drive and the land-scaped areas.

1. VISUALIZATION 101

Before you begin, step back and try to visualize how something in your garden might look. The ability to see what is possible in your mind's eye is a valuable skill that takes concerted practice to master. There are handy computer programs that help you conjure up images, but nothing replaces the speed and ease of visualization. It does take repeated practice to master this skill—I used to give myself headaches trying to "see" something on a site, but now it comes easily.

The secret to imagining how a plant bed, walk, or wall might look on an open lot or wooded slope is to remember that nothing is impossible. As Thomas Church, the great twentieth-century American landscape architect, said, "The only limit to your garden is at the boundaries of your imagination." So if you think a low-sitting wall might look good in the backyard, then try to imagine it in place. This requires staring at the spot where you are contemplating a wall. Try to see the height and length of the wall in that place. Also imagine the materials it is made from, such as stone, concrete, or blocks. Try this once a day for several days. Believe it or not, the images will eventually form in your mind. After repeated visualizations, the practice gets much easier. Soon, you will be "seeing" the changes you imagine making.

2. WHAT'S THE GOAL?

Researchers tell us that writing down a specific goal helps us to attain it. This is true in the garden too. While you may not want to draw up a design plan, you should at least declare what you aim to achieve.

This sounds fairly obvious, but stating a goal such as, "I want to create a modern, sleek outdoor space for socializing," is quite different from "I want a flower-filled, intimate patio where I can enjoy my morning coffee." To this declaration you can add the criteria of a "low-maintenance land-scape" or an "eco-friendly garden" that is pesticide free. Once you define your goal—and keep it in mind—it is easier to resist the urge to buy that Victorian wrought iron plant holder (on sale!) for your midcentury modern home.

In addition to a written or verbal declaration, you can also define your goal with the help of "wish photos." Try collecting images from garden sites on the Internet. This is a common designer technique. Images of what appeals to you are so helpful when choosing plants, furniture, and more. The goal is what defines the garden, and how strictly you implement it is up to you.

If your goal is a fall garden, make sure to add the shade-loving perennial flower, Toadlily (Tricyrtis formosana, 'Dark Beauty'). It is a star in the fall as its exuberant flowers add a lush look to any border.

The owners of this terrace garden knew their goal: lots of color and a place to enjoy their classic statuary. Here they sit amidst summer flowers such as dwarf black-eyed Susan (Rudbeckia fulgida 'Goldsturm') and white phlox (Phlox paniculata 'David') and carefully placed artful accents.

The addition of curved grass steps here created two areas in this small backyard. The separation makes the space seem larger. A planting of the green and white leaves of the variegated red twig dogwood (Cornus alba 'Elegantissima') catches the eye.

3. THE SUM IS MORE THAN ITS PARTS

Design in art is a recognition of the relation between various
things, various elements in the creative flux. —D. H. Lawrence

The overall design of your landscape is of paramount importance. All areas and elements should fit within a cohesive arrangement and no area should take precedence over the others—they should all "pull together" equally. As D. H. Lawrence said, it is "the relation between various things, various elements."

An ordered approach may make us see our yard as a large central space and nothing more. Indeed, many of us look at our yards as emptiness to be bordered with greenery. Instead, think of how your yard may be divided into sections through the strategic placement of a hedge, steps, or wall. A compelling landscape connects each area to another and lets them flow easily.

Like the fingers of your hand, the different areas of a garden should be separate but work together. This is what I mean by "the sum is more than its parts." In looking at your landscape, ask yourself if you can create different areas, such as a sitting area, an open gathering zone, and a small quiet garden spot, that lead from one to another, even if it is a small space. That is the key to a great outdoor space.

4. THE GRACEFUL SWEEP OF A CURVE

The sweep of a curve lends a gracious air to a landscape. Your eye can-not help but follow it around. By laying out a plant bed or walkway in a strong, curving line, you invite people to explore. Use a curve with a single radius to create a visual impact. Graceful arcs reflect the forms we see in nature—flower petals, pine cones, leaves, and seashells. Stay away from curvy wiggles because they dilute the captivating "follow me" effect.

An effective way to lay out an accurate curve for a plant bed is to use a 100-foot tape measure as a compass of sorts. Anchor the end of the tape at a central point, then hold the other end at a radius measurement of your choosing. Then, pivoting around, you can lay out a uniformly shaped curve to denote the arc of the radius using "marking" paint (not spray paint!) or a line of powdered limestone. The resulting curve can then be cut into the earth with a sharp spade. The gentle, curved plant bed, wall, or walk you create will provide an even "disposition" to the landscape.

Curved lines in a garden can be made with bluestone pavers that resemble a "ribbon" inserted in a lawn, as I did here.

A curved plant bed of annual flowers such as red salvia and white impatiens combines the elegance of a gracious arc with the vibrancy of color.

A curving stone walk (they also serve as tracks for a mower) bordered with pachysandra leads through a gate. The view beyond the gate is hidden and invites further exploration.

5. HIDE AND REVEAL—THE MYSTERY OF THE UNSEEN

If you want a small outdoor space to appear larger or more interesting, you can use an ancient Japanese design technique known as *miegakure,* or "hide and reveal." This technique involves partially screening a view or section of a garden with a strategically placed shrub or wall to create the illusion of distance.

By providing a half-hidden vista, you encourage people to go farther into a space. This popular garden design technique is used for making smaller yards appear larger than they are. People will invariably walk forward to see what lies ahead, unseen.

You can hide parts of your garden by planting a leafy plant by a curve, angling a set of steps, or locating a mound in front of the view. You can even plant a mass of plants to create shadows. The shade they produce "darken" an area, which makes it appear to recede in the distance.

These stone and gravel steps curve down and out of sight, beckoning you to go farther. The light color of the steps make them stand out in this shady spot and their width allows plants to grow over the edges without limiting room to walk. The evergreen arborvitae (Thuja occidentalis) on the left and the large leaves of the oakleaf hydrangea (Hydrangea quercifolia) on the right side of the steps hides what lies ahead.

6. THE PRINCIPLE OF THREE DEPTHS

You may know the meaning of the words *foreground* and *background* but have you heard of *middle ground*? Middle ground separates the front from the rear and creates a more interesting layered view. This layered view is used in Asian landscape painting. George Rowley, describes it in his book *Principles of Chinese Painting*:

> The Chinese perfected the principle of three depths according to which spatial depth was marked by a foreground, a middle distance, and far distance, each parallel to the picture plane, so that the eyes leapt from one distance to the next through a void of space.

In other words, a long view is more intriguing with something placed in a central zone where the eye can rest before going on to the background. A plant bed, planter, or hedge set within the middle area of a view increases the perceived depth of a space by providing a central reference point. This is a great tip—try placing something in the front of a valued view and see if it adds some depth and magic to the garden.

The principle of three depths is well illustrated here—in this scene, the 'Paul's Glory' hosta and Christmas ferns make up the foreground, the swinging bench is the middle ground. The long view into the woods is more interesting with the bench in the middle ground.

The lantern atop the rock is the foreground, the overhanging tree is the middle ground, and the waterfall is the background.

7. FIND THE POWER SPOT

Every garden contains what I call a power spot. This is a place that, for some reason, seems a little more interesting than anywhere else on the site. A high section of lawn, a spot beneath a large tree, or a half-hidden rock can become the power spot. The choice is yours. The feeling you get when you stand there will let you know if a spot is special. High points and elevated locations such as the top of a slope can feel exalted while a shaded corner may feel more familiar. You can choose both if you want.

To find a power spot, walk around and simply notice how you feel while standing there. You may choose to linger there longer than anywhere else. There is no right or wrong answer—it is your personal determination.

You can name it to make it extra special, like The Lone Oak or Rock of the Mountain King. Have fun with it. It is time for the power spot of your garden to be revealed!

These amazing boulders were hidden by weedy growth and construction debris that was thrown there. The homeowner uncovered them and added some ostrich ferns and Christmas ferns (Polystichum acrostichoides) at the base. Now his grandkids play in this magical "power spot."

8. FRAMING A GARDEN

We live in a world of rectangular living spaces. Our houses, buildings, and rooms are more likely to be a rectangle than any other shape. That is why so many of us prefer rectangular outdoor spaces. We are familiar with straight lines and 90-degree corners and are comforted by the simplicity of rectilinear lines.

Rectangular outdoor areas such as terraces, lawn areas, or plant beds impose a certain kind of order on a landscape. You can create a rectangular frame to a space by adding low walls or plant beds. Below, in the garden on the right, I framed a rectangular lawn with a wall. One side is much longer than the other and is the more dominant line. In such a situation make sure the corners are exactly 90 degrees. Precision is very important in this kind of layout.

When you frame a garden using plant beds, you can plant geometric hedges of evergreen plants to reinforce it. Or you can use soft plants to contrast with the formal lines of the plant bed, as shown.

Left: *The clean, straight lines of the plant beds create a "frame" around the lawn. A mass of purple 'Rozanne' geraniums* (Geranium x *'Rozanne'*) *and 'Little Lime' hydrangeas* (Hydrangea paniculata *'Little Lime'®*) *adds color from the summer into the fall.*

Right: *The low stone wall makes a defined boundary, and the resulting outdoor space invites activity. Everyone likes to sit on the wall in the corner.*

9. BLEND LIGHT AND SHADOW

We all enjoy dappled shade where the shadows dance beneath open-branched trees. The sunlight appears as drops of light on the ground, moving and changing. This play of light catches our attention. Think about varying the types of light and shadow in your garden when planting or pruning.

Dappled shade is different from partial shade. Dappled shade is when sunlight is filtered through high branches of deciduous trees with smaller leaves. It forms a mosaic of light and shadow through the day. Partial shade may mean sunlight in the morning and shade in the afternoon, which is a very different situation. Many plants, like people, like the filtered light of dappled shade. It appeals to us because we associate dappled light with a comfortable place to sit out of the bright sun.

Also consider the alluring effect of deep shade at the edges of a garden. As you travel farther from the central area, plant trees and shrubs a little more closely together. These shady zones blur the edges of a space and provide a sense of mystery.

By planting one large tree in a lawn area you can create a special shady zone within an open sunny area. The experience of sitting in the shade looking out onto a bright open area is especially wonderful on a hot summer day.

We don't always notice the light and shadows in a landscape but they affect us silently. Here, the sunlight is filtered through the leaves of a multi-stem Heritage® river birch (Betula nigra 'Cully') onto the plants below. The sunlight falls like dancing drops of light.

10. HAVE A SEAT—ADIRONDACK CHAIRS

A garden is a relaxing antidote to our fast-paced world. Where else can we simply sit and enjoy the sunshine and air and listen to the birds? An outdoor chair that has a gentle recline and wide armrests (for that glass of iced tea) encourages us to enjoy the atmosphere. Just the sight of such a casual chair makes us want to stop and take a seat. So why not consider getting a classic Adirondack chair or two for your garden?

The first Adirondack chair was created by Thomas Lee in 1903 for his summer cottage near the Adirondack Mountains of upstate New York. It was made from wood and was somewhat rustic. Over the years, the chair has been widely modified in details and materials but, despite these adaptations, Adirondack chairs are remarkably recognizable and persistently popular. They are simple, useful, and comfortable. They are available in wood or synthetic materials and are adaptable to any style of landscape.

In short, Adirondack chairs are a classic. They signify summertime leisure just by their mere presence in a garden. And you can have fun painting them in colors or even fun motifs. Have a seat!

Adirondack chairs are now made of slats of wood instead of the single plank of the original chair Thomas Lee created in 1903. There is a wide range of choices when it comes to Adirondack chairs today. Variations include flared rear backrests, different top treatments, and modern materials such as 100-percent recycled polyethylene.

11. EAST—DIRECTION OF GROWTH AND RENEWAL

East, the home of the morning sun, is considered by many cultures to be an auspicious direction, encouraging growth and renewal. Plants wake up with the sun and do their best growing in the gentle rays of morning that come from the east. This is especially true for flowers that have tender petals such as roses and clematis. The dew that forms overnight dries quickly in the morning sun, and flowers last longer in mild morning light than they do in the hot afternoon sun. Wise gardeners know this and site their vegetable and rose plots to get maximum eastern exposure.

We are like plants in that east is beneficial for us too. *Vastu*, the ancient Indian teachings on the design of the environment, maintains that we think better when we face east. These teachings suggest buildings should face east. The word *orientation* means to face east, and it's used for siting a building or plant bed.

If you know that an eastern outlook may enhance your mental processes, then orient garden benches so that they face east.

East is the direction the ancient cultures favored over the others. Many ancient buildings, churches, and temples face east and many of the great libraries had large windows to the east. An example of this is the main branch of the New York Public Library located at 42nd Street and 5th Avenue in New York City.

Gardentopia

Flowers like the eastern sun in the morning. Here white zinnias seem to reach for the light by turning toward the east ever so slightly.

We exposed these wonderful rocks and built some stone walls near them. They are representative of the natural environment and attest to the fascinating geological history of the area.

12. RESPECT THE GENIUS OF THE PLACE

In the 1700s, the English poet Alexander Pope urged owners of country estates to cast aside whims of fancy in their landscaping projects. He advised them to enhance the inherent qualities of the land and wrote this in his "Epistle to Lord Burlington":

> To build, to plant, whatever you intend,
> To rear the column, or the arch to bend,
> To swell the terrace, or to sink the grot;
> In all, let Nature never be forgot. . . .
> Consult the genius of the place in all . . .

There is no more important garden tip than this! Today, we are rediscovering the truth of taking inspiration from nature itself. By respecting the genius of a place, you highlight the natural setting rather than alter it. If you are working with a rocky site, instead of removing the rocks or covering them up, you can expose rock outcrops in a way that showcases them. If you have a grand tree, you can highlight its magnificence by clearing the space around it.

By working in tune with the intelligent rhythm of nature you are honoring its processes instead of trampling on them. A steep hill can be planted and become a mural of sorts. A flat lawn can be transformed into an undulating sea of grasses. This sensitive approach spotlights the "genius" of the place.

13. CAPTURE THE VIEW BEYOND

In Japan, they use a design technique called "borrowed scenery" to make a small outdoor space more interesting. This technique incorporates a view of a feature that lies beyond the garden to carry the eye outward. Following this technique, you can "borrow" a view of a distant building, a peek into neighboring woods, or just a neighbor's nearby tree.

In order to borrow scenery, you may have to trim a hedge to a certain height so you can see over it. Or you might have to cut back the branches of a wide-spreading tree in order to reveal something beyond it. I call this opening the vista. Look outside; is there something beyond your boundaries that is worth revealing? Perhaps it is a neighbor's Japanese maple or the view of a distant hill.

Don't forget to look down too. The borrowed scenery may be a low-growing azalea or yucca. The Japanese have four categories of borrowed scenery that relates to location:

I trimmed back this red-leaved Japanese maple to reveal the front door. Its color almost matches the fall color of the tree—another reason to borrow that view! It would be more effective if the evergreen holly on the right were also trimmed back. This would allow the borrowed scenery to be more noticeable.

Far—a view of a distant mountain or similar landscape feature

Near—a feature just beyond a fence

High—looking up above the trees

Low—something low or something seen through an opening

14. MUSHROOMS AND STADDLE STONES

Stone or concrete mushrooms are popular garden accents because their rounded, natural form is so familiar and makes us smile. And they can fit in anywhere. Mushrooms of varying sizes can be placed in a plant bed, set as markers along a walk, or used to emphasize an entrance. They are a fun addition to a landscape and are enhanced when flowers, ferns, sedum, or low groundcovers grow around them.

If you want an authentic mushroom shape in the garden, look for an antique staddle stone. The word *staddle* comes from the Old English word, *stathol*, for base. Staddle stones were used in medieval Europe to raise small elevated structures that held grain or other foodstuffs. The unique shape of the staddle stones prevented rodents from climbing up into the granaries. Usually made of granite or sandstone, they consist of two stones—one is a 2- to 3-feet-high pedestal base, and the other is a rounded, carved stone cap that is set on top. These unique pieces were crafted by hand, so the markings on the stone are distinctive. Antique staddle stones are much valued and are increasingly hard to find.

A staddle stone features the chisel marks of a mason's handiwork. It catches the eye and offers contrast in a plant bed containing 'Anthony Waterer' spirea (Spirea bumalda 'Anthony Waterer') and 'All Gold' Japanese forest grass (Hakonechloa macra 'All Gold').

15. POWER OF THE PORTAL

Portals are an effective way to highlight an entrance into a garden. They act as a kind of marker or feature that people walk through. By adding a gate, an arch, or just two vertical posts that visitors pass between, you subtly announce a shift in atmosphere. This is what I mean by "the power of the portal"—it is an opening that signifies a transition from one space into another. Like a garden gate that beckons visitors to a cottage, a simple portal says, "Welcome."

The use of an entry marker is nothing new. Gates and arches have long been used in landscapes around the world. In Japan, visitors enter the grounds of Shinto shrines by passing beneath a red wooden structure called a torii. In Europe, historic ceremonial stone arches announce entry into a grand garden. Today, you can enhance the entry into your garden by adding a gate and an overhead pergola.

Another portal idea for a home garden is to create an opening through a living border, be it hedges or shrubs. Remember to make the opening wide enough so that people can pass through easily, and be sure to prune it regularly.

A classic white picket gate and overhead pergola is a favorite in the home landscape. The lattice side panels of the pergola frame the entrance and announce the transition into a special outdoor space. The white blooming Kousa dogwood (Cornus kousa) adds to the effect.

A stone finial adds character to the top of a wall and looks appropriate when placed at a corner or by some steps. You can add small stones next to it, as seen here. You can get finials from a stone supply yard—they come in all sizes.

Below: 'Sulphur Heart' Persian ivy (Hedera colchica 'Sulphur Heart') has large, green leaves irregularly splashed with yellow or light green. It is fast growing and vigorous and is an excellent wall climber. It makes a great accent.

16. SOFTEN A CORNER

Sharp corners of walls, especially those constructed of stone or concrete, may appear harsh in a garden. A 90-degree corner casts what Chinese feng shui calls cutting chi, or what some call a poison arrow. If you stand in the aim of this energetic arrow you may not feel as serene and relaxed as you might otherwise feel.

To counteract this unwelcome effect, you can soften sharp corners of protruding walls by planting a clinging vine that adheres by discs or rootlets. Examples of this are Boston ivy (*Parthenocissus tricuspidata*), Persian ivy (*Hedera colchica*), and Virginia creeper (*Parthenocissus quinquefolia*). I also like to plant climbing hydrangea (*Hydrangea petiolaris*) for its white summer flowers. Another favorite of mine is Rose Sensation™ False Hydrangea Vine (*Schizophragma hydrangeoides* Rose Sensation™).

In addition to a vine, I like to place a round sphere on top of the corner to soften its sharp edge. The look of a rounded form counteracts the 90-degree angle. I often use concrete or stone finials, but any spherical element is fine—even a painted bowling ball can work well.

Here a corner of a wall is softened by a round, stone finial placed atop it and by English ivy that clings to the walls. These two together minimize an angular corner very effectively.

17. WATCH OUT FOR RUNWAY LIGHTS

Outdoor lighting has recently undergone a revolution with the addition of low-voltage LED light fixtures. These are popular because they are relatively inexpensive to install and use. Before you add any lights, consider carefully where you intend to place your fixtures so that you can avoid the "runway effect."

Homeowners, with the best of intentions, often locate outdoor light fixtures every 6 feet along the side of a front walk in order to adequately light the entire way to the front door. But evenly spacing similar fixtures creates a linear light pattern that resembles an airport runway. This can be made worse if you place lights on both sides of an entry walk, because then it really looks like a landing strip.

A better solution is to place just one or a few fixtures along a walk and to illuminate the destination a little brighter. This follows the adage that says we all head toward the light. For example, place two path light fixtures on either side of a front door landing and one or two along a walk. Another option is to skip the lights altogether and use a post light at the beginning of a walk and bright lights by the door.

The light fixture should not expose the actual bulb because it appears as an overly bright spot of light in a sea of darkness. This is why fixtures with overhanging hoods are preferred over other styles. The hood directs the light onto the ground where it casts a pool of light over a general area.

'Chanticleer' Callery pears (Pyrus callervana 'Chanticleer'), an upright-pyramidal tree, are spaced in a row in front of a retaining wall. The spacing imposes order upon the landscape and reinforces the long line of the wall.

18. RE-RE-REPETITION IN THE LANDSCAPE

To make a point, repeat yourself. This is certainly true in an outdoor setting, no matter its size. A straight line featuring a repeating element in a garden makes a strong statement. The visual cue of uniformly spaced trees, pavers, or planters establishes a rhythm that ties a large space together. It can also make an outdoor area or walk more interesting. Feel free to use as many similar items in a row as you want.

Repetition in a landscape also makes it more harmonious. The view of similar elements, spaced in a predictable pattern, is easy to "read" and makes a landscape visually defined. A line of trees, shrubs, or garden accents is a layout that we all understand. The predictability is soothing to many of us and we relax within its orderly embrace.

Place a line of the same planters along a walk or up a series of steps. Or locate three or four similar chairs, in a row, in front of an evergreen screen. Or install a line of 2-by-3-inch stone pavers, equally spaced, in the lawn. Have fun with repeating elements in your garden.

Left: *Who says a row has to be straight? A repeating element in a curve here is the graceful yellow 'All Gold' Japanese forest grass* (Hakonechloa macra *'All Gold') fronted by the dark green groundcover, 'Bowles' myrtle* (Vinca minor *'Bowles'). The golden blades of this hardy, deer-resistant plant look great in repetition.*

Right: *I placed an evenly spaced row of terra cotta planters, filled with gravel to maintain stability, in front of a backdrop of white pine trees* (Pinus strobus). *The pines are pruned to help the repetition stand out.*

19. A WINDOW IN THE GARDEN

A window of any kind in the garden frames a view. This window can take many forms. It may be an opening cut through a wall of flowering plants, a vista seen through an open gate, a view down a long path flanked by overhanging trees, or a scene viewed through an actual rectangular frame softened by creeping fig or ivy. The view framed by an opening directs a person's attention outward to highlight something special, be it a distant tree or a single rose up close. Such a garden window focuses attention on a particular area and creates a sense of depth as it emphasizes something that might not be obvious.

If you would like to add a window in your landscape, first decide where the best views are located. You may have a view that looks great in spring and another that is wonderful in winter. If that is the case, why not include two windows for seasonal viewing? The spring window can be a view through a garden gate looking out onto your deutzias, lilacs, or azaleas. The winter window can be a long view, through two trees, out to conifers and rhododendrons.

This tip also applies to the view from the real windows in your house. Don't neglect how the garden looks from indoors—that is one of the most important views of all.

The view through a stone doorway in Chanticleer, a public garden in Wayne, Pennsylvania, directs the eye out to a distant garden.

The green "window" shown here is at the Tuin de Villa in Persingen, the Netherlands. Designed by owners Lily and Fried Frederix. Photo by Laura McKillop.

Below: *This rustic wood bench at the public garden, Wave Hill, in the Bronx in New York City, also includes a "window" above the backrest. This ingenious design frames the view into the wooded area beyond the flower garden. It draws you forward to look through the window.*

Add a rustic portal to a woodland garden for a sense of arrival. Here perennial geraniums and ferns form a green setting to a rough cedar arbor in the garden of a cherished clients. It was built by David Robinson of Natural Edge (www.naturaledgerustic.com).

20. RUSTIC ELEGANCE IN A WOODED LANDSCAPE

Woodland gardens are characterized by trees, dappled light, and a hushed atmosphere. You can make such sylvan gardens even more inviting by adding a rustic seat within the setting. A wooden bench, crafted from bent branches of red cedar, willow, Osage orange, laurel, or other woody plants evokes a sturdy elegance amidst natural surroundings.

Consider the location of your bench carefully. Find a spot where people might want to stop and sit. In a wooded area, this can be a clearing where sunlight seeps through the trees or where a view is possible. A rustic bench will feel more sheltered when backed by plantings or large trees. And last, do not place the bench in a low point where water might collect. No one wants to sit in a soggy spot.

I like to set a bench on a cleared area so that people's feet are not touched by grass or vegetation. If you want the area to be special, you can add a few flat stones or some compacted gravel beneath the bench. Make sure it extends out in front of the bench to accommodate people's feet.

A bent willow seat sits nicely in a shady niche among hosta and bigroot geranium (Geranium macrorrhizum *Bevan's Variety). I planted tall yews behind it. The sheltered location makes it even more inviting.*

21. IRRESISTIBLE LOOKOUTS

Is there a slope in your yard with an opportunity for a view? A lookout is one of the most exciting areas in a landscape. Elevated locations such as a hilltop or a rock outcrop can serve as a "prospect" where you can stop and enjoy a view. It seems we all have that urge to climb a slope and look out from a high point upon the scene below.

An outlook can be on a small rise or on a dramatic hilltop. You may have to prune some trees or shrubs in order to reveal a vista. You may also need to level out a small area at the top of a high point to create a place suitable for a sitting rock or bench. You might even have to build a path or steps leading up to the overlook point. But all that work will be worth it because, once you get to the top, a lovely view awaits! For a brief time, you will be lord of all you survey. I think this enjoyable feeling is what lies behind the allure of a lookout. It is irresistible.

Lookouts and overlooks all share one thing in common: a high perch. You must be able to look down on the view below. It can be a view of a garden, a town, hills, or something else. The two examples shown here look down on a watery view.

Rocky outcrops can be transformed into a tantalizing garden with the addition of a groundcover like the tough Goldmoss sedum (Sedum acre). Here it trails over the rocks showing off its clusters of yellow, star-shaped flowers in spring. Down in front, a clump of sky-blue flowers of 'Blue Storm' agapanthus (Agapanthus praecox orientalis 'Blue Storm') is highlighted by the dark gray backdrop.

22. SHOW OFF THAT ROCK!

*There is life in a stone. Any stone that sits in a field or lies on a
beach takes on the memory of that place. —Andy Goldsworthy*

Rocks are not inert. They resonate with the energy of a place, and they
provide a stabilizing presence in a garden. This truth was known in the
ancient cultures of Asia, Australia, Europe, and the Americas where
unusual rocks were revered. The Japanese have a tradition of categoriz-
ing natural rocks according to their character, appearance, and origin.
Stone is a prized element in their gardens, and they are used to represent
strength, eternity, mountains, and much more.

If you unearth a boulder that you find interesting, clean it off and
make it a garden feature. Shine a spotlight on it or plant near it. Showing
off an unusual boulder or outcrop helps us appreciate nature—and our
time with her—with a little more reverence.

*Certain rocks can resemble water, fire, trees, or other natural elements. Here a rock has
marked ridges that resemble licks of flames. Such a "fire" rock, sitting solitary on the earth,
can add character to any garden. This unusual rock is one of several outstanding boulders
you can see at the public garden, Innisfree, in Millbrook, New York.*

23. PLANTER IN A BED

Even when you think your garden feels finished, it never is. There is always something more to do. For example, when your plants are grown and the plant beds are filled, that is when you can place a large pot of flowers within that bed. The contrast of flowers above the foliage makes quite a lovely sight. Conversely, place a planter filled with bold foliage within a flower-filled bed. The effect of large leaf plants such as caladiums or hosta is tantalizing when they stand above a bed of wax begonias (*Begonia semperflorens*) or 'Rozanne' perennial geraniums (*Geranium* 'Rozanne'). And in warm areas try a large pot full of Fox Tail Agave (*Agave attenuata*) with its bold rosette foliage.

The style of the flowerpot that you use is not that important because it will be partially hidden by greenery. Just remember that it needs to be watered. Use a long wand with an appropriate watering nozzle on your hose to better reach the pot, if necessary. And don't forget to elevate the pot by placing it atop a brick, block, or flat rock. This helps it sit above the surrounding plants so that it can be more noticeable. It also helps with drainage of the pot.

Left: *I created this garden for a dear client and, after a few years, I placed this planter on a base within the plant bed. The spring flowers shown here add a dash of color. It is right by their door.*

Below: *This planter sits among an exuberant planting. It can be seen at the entrance to Coastal Maine Botanical Gardens in Boothbay Harbor, Maine.*

This arbor at the Huntington Botanical Gardens in San Marino, California, is an example of how the lines of a walk seem to get closer the farther away they are. This is an aspect of perspective.

24. TRICKING THE EYE

In a perspective view, the lines of a long walk seem to converge. If you look closely you will see that the farther away the lines of the walk are, the closer they appear to each other. Learning how to manipulate this visual illusion is something that all art students learn about when they study perspective. Likewise, you can use the visual trick of converging lines to create an appearance of distance in any outdoor space.

This trick of perspective can make a small outdoor space appear larger than it actually is. For example, if you have a short but straight walk that leads to an area, you can make the walk appear longer by slightly angling the lines inward. The key word here is *slightly*, because if the angle is too sharp then the effect is noticeable. You can use the same technique with a plant bed. Again, angle the lines inward very slightly so it appears as a natural perspective. The converging lines are a visual cue that makes the plant bed look longer than it is in reality.

You can also apply this trick to a rectangular lawn area. If the bed lines that border the lawn angle inward, the lawn will seem to be a little deeper than it really is.

I used this trick in this stony dry stream. It appears longer because it narrows at one end and is covered in foliage.

25. RECLAIM AN OLD METAL GATE

A unique metal gateway makes an entry into a garden special. Right from the beginning you know you are entering another world. So why not go on a gate hunt to find something distinctive? You can look for an old gate or repurpose something to become a gate. Visit salvage yards and antique shops, or search the Internet for a one-of-a-kind gate. You never know what you might find.

Tip: Do not pass by that old, rusty iron gate without giving it a second look. Try to imagine how it might look all cleaned up. Or investigate a salvaged metal window grille to see how it can be modified to be used as a gate. With a little love—and a lot of elbow grease—either option can become a memorable backyard entry feature. A local ironwork company can help you attach hinges and latches to your new gate.

When working with iron, removing all of the rust is important. Once the rust is removed, add a fresh coat of paint with a rust-resistant finish. Or, instead of paint, you can rub on an automobile paste wax to keep the metal from rusting. This extra effort will be well worth it, as the rescued gate featured here demonstrates.

This antique, double gate was rusted and sitting in a forgotten outside corner when we found it. It was restored and now serves as an entry to an intimate, enclosed garden.

26. WHY WE LOVE ROUNDED FORMS IN THE GARDEN

Rounded shapes such as curved pots and sculptures are often found in our landscapes. Why is this? What is it about rounded forms that appeal to us? Perhaps rounded forms remind us of home and family. Or maybe they hark back to organic shapes, such as fruit, seeds, or eggs. It also could be that we are "wired" to prefer rounded shapes.

Scientists at the Zanvyl Krieger Mind/Brain Institute found that people prefer shapes with gentle curves as opposed to those with sharp points. In fact, the magnetic brain-imaging scans they conducted showed that rounded shapes produce stronger responses and increased activity in the brain. Rounded shapes aroused the brain while sharp points did not.

Eric Jaffe, writing in the business magazine *Fast Company*, says our preference for this shape may be hardwired in our brains, saying, "Roundness seems to be a universal human pleasure." In fact, researchers found that our eyes record a curve faster than we process corners. It takes less work for us to recognize rounded forms than hard edge shapes. We are made for curved elements.

So add something round into your garden and see the effect of it for yourself.

Top: *We placed this rounded pot in a woodland garden after all danger of frost passed. The rounded shape looks great next to blooming white azaleas.*

Bottom: *A rounded, deep red urn evokes warm feelings as it sits in a partially shaded plant bed accompanied by white hydrangea and green-and-white 'Patriot' hosta. The weathered markings on the urn make it more interesting. You can see this at the New York Botanical Garden.*

27. THE INTRIGUING DRY STREAM

An attractive drainage solution for eliminating puddles in a lawn is to direct surface runoff into a dry stream. Also referred to as a dry creek, this landscape feature is a gravel-filled trench that is laid out to look like a natural watercourse. It does not normally hold water but simply allows it to permeate down into the earth. A dry stream is easy to install and looks beautiful when bordered with rocks and low-growing plants. Locate this feature at the edge of a grassy area to catch runoff from the lawn.

To create a dry stream, first paint out the layout of the stream on the ground. Make it slightly curving with wider sections so that it appears natural. Then dig out the soil to make a sloped trench that is at least 12 inches wide and about 12 inches deep. As you dig, mound the excavated soil on the far side of the stream bed to make it higher than the side where people walk. This makes it easier to show off the plants that will be planted there. Line the trench with filter fabric (not plastic!). Place rocks along both sides of the stream bed. Fill the trench with coarse gravel to within 4 inches of the top. Place a layer of rounded stones on top of the gravel. Last, create plant beds on the far side of the dry stream and a few along the bank where people are standing, and then fill the beds with low-growing plants.

Before-and-after photos of a dry stream illustrate how the lines of the trench curve like a natural stream. This is in my backyard and I chose plants that would normally grow by a stream such as Siberian iris (Iris sibirica) and the yellow and white 'Evergold' sedge (Carex oshimensis 'Evergold'). The purple flowers are 'Buddy Purple' Gomphrena.

28. YIN AND YANG IN THE GARDEN

Traditional Chinese gardens embrace the idea of yin and yang. This philosophy describes two opposites that, together, form a harmonious whole. A yang element is hard, lighter colored, or vertical. A yin element is soft, darker colored, or rounded. The contrast of these two attributes is at the heart of great garden design.

You need both yin and yang areas to create a satisfying landscape. Sunny open areas are yang. Contained shady spots are yin. A combination of both are best for a complete experience. Additionally, the counterpoint of hard rocks (yang) and soft water (yin), light colors (yang) and dark leaves (yin), generates a subtle tension that uplifts any garden.

Rocks, a hard yang element, symbolize the timelessness of mountains. Soft foliage, which is yin, suggests the never-ending cycles of nature. You can employ yin and yang in any number of ways. You can set a light-colored hard rock against the soft, airy foliage of a laceleaf Japanese maple. You can also contrast small gravel against large leaves. Or you can place dark-leaved plants against light green ones. Out of contrast and complementarity, harmony is born.

Hard rock is considered "yang." Soft leaves, flowers. and water are considered "yin." The juxtaposition of hard and soft creates a visual counterpoint. Here is yin and yang in its varieties in a garden.

29. ACCESSORIZING YOUR GARDEN
WITH POT FEET

Pot feet are a little-known accessory for elevating planters off the ground. They are used to ensure that containers get adequate drainage. Place three or four pot feet, spaced evenly, under a planter to raise it slightly. This allows water to exit easily and prevents the plants from becoming waterlogged. Pot feet also aid in air circulation and prevent mold from growing under the pot, which can mark up a deck or terrace. They make a big difference in the health and growth of the plants in containers. I always use them for these reasons.

You can buy ready-made pot feet that are decorative and match the planter. For example, a terra cotta pot would have terra cotta pot feet. But you can use whatever works. Try placing plastic bottle caps, small rocks, or flat glass "pebbles" under a large pot to raise it off the ground. You can even use old bricks.

One cautionary note—consider a plant's moisture requirements before using pot feet. Some moisture-loving plants, like certain semi-tropicals, like the water and may not appreciate any additional drainage.

Left: *Pot feet add an elegant touch to an ornate planter. They can match the pot in materials and style, making a decorative statement, as shown here.*

Right: *The purple petunias, dark pink Callibrachoas, and tall yellow flowers in this planter would not be thriving if they did not have the added drainage supplied by pot feet.*

A soft mulched, long view in a flower garden by Brooke Beebe

30. THE LONG VIEW

Long, straight views inexorably lead the eye. You cannot help but follow a straight line in the garden to its end. Therefore, find the lengthiest straight line you can in an outdoor space and use it to its best advantage. A long view may involve looking diagonally across your yard or down a slope. You do not have to have a large yard, just use whatever length you have for the proverbial long view.

Russell Page, the celebrated twentieth-century English landscape designer, wrote about creating long views in his wonderful book *The Education of a Gardener* (first published in 1962):

> Where a site suggests to me a long straight axis, I try to keep this axis as narrow as I can, proportionately to the area I have to deal with. . . . Such straight lines focus the attention and give direction to a garden design—you may interpret them in a hundred different ways.

Page's suggestion to keep the long axis narrow can be applied to a garden walk, pool, or plant bed. The narrower it is, the longer it will appear.

Walking here, you can enjoy the flower border of deer-resistant white Angelonia 'Serena' and blue Ageratum, but your eye goes straight to the gate and steps at the end.

31. EXCLAMATION POINTS—COLUMNAR PLANTS, PILLARS, AND POLES

Sometimes a garden needs a vertical "punch" to add some drama. A tall, narrow pole or spire, thrusting upward, perhaps at a slight angle, can shatter the placid face of a landscape. Narrow trees such as the 'Slender Silhouette' American sweetgum (*Liquidambar styraciflua* 'Slender Silhouette'), or columnar shrubs such as 'Sky Pencil' Japanese holly (*Ilex crenata* 'Sky Pencil') can be used as a natural spire, injecting contrast in a plant bed. Even simple cedar posts painted red insert some "rudeness" into a setting, appearing as trunks of some exotic trees.

Pointed, vertical structures can be fashioned from wood, metal, branches, or even rebar. A pyramidal pillar, called an obelisk, or *tuteur*, is a traditional garden element. It is often topped with a round finial or copper cap for effect. The size and shape of these versatile accents may vary—you can place a tall obelisk in a flowerbed or insert a shorter one into a large planter.

Another eye-catching option is to set an individual pole or a tall stone into a landscape. They work well in small urban spaces, cottage gardens, and formal modern settings. Tall poles can support lanky morning glories or trailing clematis. Or they can be left unadorned and act as a focal point. The historic estate garden, Naumkeag, in Stockbridge, Massachusetts (open to the public), has 17 carved, Venetian gondola poles surrounding a terrace garden. It makes a memorable sight.

Top, left: *A red painted cedar post, one of several, stands in front of a red-berried viburnum at Jack Lenor Larsen's LongHouse Reserve in Easthampton, New York. Open to the public.*

Top, right: *A dense and columnar 'Sky Pencil' Japanese holly (*Ilex crenata *'Sky Pencil') makes a great contrast to the loosely spreading, red-leaved smokebush.*

Bottom, left: *I created a red vertical accent here with three trellis poles. I painted them a fire engine red. They add a dynamic spark to this outdoor sitting area.*

Bottom, right: *You can insert pointed features, known as* tuteurs, *in a plant bed as they did in the wondrous garden at the public garden, Stonecrop, in Cold Spring, New York. The pointed pillars add vertical interest to the yellow tulips and more that grow around them.*

32. PLACING A WATER CASCADE—ELEVATE AND SET BACK

Many people love the idea of a recirculating water cascade outside their home. A submersible pump, hidden in the base of the falls, pumps the water back to the top. It is not that hard to install and can look quite dramatic. But there are a few pointers you should consider before building a waterfall in your landscape:

- Do not locate a cascade too close to the house because the sound may be heard indoors. I have seen this mistake, and the end result was that the homeowners could not run the cascade very often because it was too loud.

- The top of the cascade should start above eye level. This draws the viewer's eye upward and creates a dramatic scene.

- Set the top of the falls farther back and allow the water to fall and come closer to the viewer. This makes the waterfall appear to recede in the distance. You can also narrow the watercourse at the top to make it look longer.

- To make the cascade appear to be farther away, plant a few dark evergreens behind and to the side of the waterfall. A dark background recedes and therefore the effect is that the cascade seems farther away.

Left: *The water gushing out of the top of the recirculating cascade here travels down a steep drop to create a dramatic scene. I planted the shade-loving, yellow Corydalis (Corydalis lutea) to add a soft touch with its ferny foliage and bright yellow, spurred flowers. It blooms from May to September.*

Opposite page: *When you lay out a cascade don't forget to include several turns as I did here. The top of this one is set back and may be slightly obscured by tall foliage in front. This hide-and-reveal technique helps it appear longer than it really is.*

33. CIRCLES IN THE LANDSCAPE

We all respond positively to a circle's perfect form. It is the universal symbol of completeness. In a landscape, a circular shape makes a powerful statement and promotes harmony and connection. Since the earliest of times, various cultures have incorporated circles into their parks and gardens. A good example of this is the Native American council ring, a round outdoor meeting area where people came to discuss important matters.

A circle in the landscape always directs our attention to the center point. A landscape circle, such as an island in a driveway or a round rose garden, often has a prominent feature placed in the middle, like a tree or a fountain. This type of feature makes sense because it works so well with a circular shape.

A circular area of paving is a great way to unify a space. It is an effective connector for several walks coming from different directions. As Carl Jung, the Swiss psychologist, said, the circle "is the exponent of all paths."

Top: *A circular stone "council ring" in the Azalea Garden at the New York Botanical Garden beckons you to enter and sit at its perimeter.*

Bottom: *A circular shape can be a unifying connector for walks in a landscape, as I designed it here. The contrast of bricks and bluestone also adds interest.*

34. RAIN CHAINS

Rain chains provide functional and unique accents to a landscape. They are used in place of a closed downspout to direct water from a roof gutter. These decorative chains, which consist of simple links or a series of cups in a vertical line, are made from copper, brass, or rust-resistant aluminum. Catch basins at the ground level contain the rainwater and direct the water away. They can match a wide range of architectural styles.

The Japanese developed the rain chain and have used them for centuries. They value them for their visual appeal and also for the varied sounds the rainwater makes as it travels down the length of the chain. This "rainwater music" can vary from the tinkling of droplets to the soft rush of rainwater. Rain chains are a delight to hear.

The incentive to replace a downspout with a rain chain is enhanced if you want to harvest rainwater and direct it into a rain barrel. This makes rain chains part of a sustainable landscape. Other catchment options include a gravel-filled basin or drain that is below ground.

Note the green tones of the verdigris on the rain chain—it is the natural patina that forms on copper or brass when it weathers over a period of time.

A simple rain chain made of round links.

35. THE LURE OF THE SHELTERED CORNER

Did you ever notice that the most desirable place to sit outside is where you have your back to a tree, a wall, or a hedge while you face a view? People love to sit in a protected corner, looking out. This is at the heart of a site design technique that I call, "The Lure of a Sheltered Corner." Knowing this, you can create a spot in your garden where everyone will want to sit.

Christopher Alexander writes about making a snug sitting spot in his classic book, *A Pattern Language*:

> In the very smallest of outdoor spaces, in private gardens, this pattern tells you to make a corner of the space as a "back" with a seat, looking out on the garden. If it is rightly made, this corner will be snug, but not at all claustrophobic.

You can create such a place if you use the rear wall of a house to act as one side of this protected area and add a low hedge, perpendicular to the wall, to form the other side. The quiet enjoyment of this corner sanctuary will be enhanced if you can see a portion of your garden from here.

Looking out to a beautiful view with a wall and rock outcrop to your back is the sweetest place to sit outdoors. The chaise lounges are placed here for that reason.

Top, left: *A small stone frog sits atop a ball within 'Blue Rug' juniper (Juniperus horizontalis 'Wiltonii') and beneath a Dragon's Eye Japanese Red Pine (Pinus densiflora 'Oculus Draconis'). The small creature is an unexpected surprise!*

Top, right: *For fun, this garden owner placed a colorful lizard in a shady hosta bed. Everyone smiles when they see it.*

Left: *Place a pineapple finial within a bed of lavender ageratum as a welcoming accent.*

36. ARTFUL ACCENTS—WHERE TO PLACE THEM?

An outdoor accent or feature can personalize your garden and make it uniquely yours. If placed correctly, an interesting sculpture can add surprise or playfulness to a scene. For example, set a whimsical figure where you least expect it—in the shadows by a walk, peeking out from some shrubs, or hanging from tree branches. People love this kind of surprise.

Other fun locations for a garden accent are by an entry gate or at the top of some steps. Both locations allow people to see it up close. If the accent has an evergreen backdrop of some sort it will really stand out.

A large planter or urn can be used as a focal point. It can be located at the end of a straight walk or in a far corner of a lawn. This draws the eye and extends the perceived depth of the area. To highlight its importance, you can elevate the accent by setting it on a concrete base or rock. This is especially suitable for a Buddha statue or a lantern.

Just a word of caution, resist the urge to place too many accents in your garden. A few make a statement, but too many can make a crowded and confusing setting.

37. POOLING AND CHANNELING

People move through space in the same way that water flows. Just as water flows rapidly through a narrow channel, we walk fast along a narrow walk. And just as water slows down as it flows into a wider pool, we slow our pace as we enter into a larger area. This site design technique is called pooling and channeling. You can see it used to great effect if you ever visit Disney World, where pooling and channeling is used as a great way to direct and control how people move through a space. Moorish gardens in southern Spain also use pooling and channeling very beautifully.

You can see how this works for yourself by watching how people walk fast down a 3-foot-wide walk and then slow down or pause when they arrive at a wider front door landing. It never fails that people pause when they reach the larger area.

When you lay out a walk, think about a spot where you might want people to stop and enjoy a view. At this point, widen the walk to create a larger area for people to pause. You can also widen the intersection where two walkways meet. Place some chairs or a bench there to invite your visitors to stay a little longer.

Top: *The grassed walk, or "channel," leads to a fenced-in round overlook. The stone paving and the round shape of the "pool" invites people to pause and look down into the wooded slope below.*

Bottom: *This brick walk flows like a channeled stream into a larger pool at the end. A stately white bench acts as a beacon and signals that this area is a stopping point. This is a great example of pooling and channeling.*

Lightweight metal chairs come in all shapes and colors. The red chairs, above, are in the public garden, Innisfree, in Millbrook, New York.

38. MOVE THE FURNITURE

The ability to easily move a chair in and out of the sun will make you more likely to use it. This is an obvious but important finding that affects the design of public parks and botanical gardens. The flexibility of light-weight and moveable furniture makes an outdoor setting more user-friendly. In fact, certain public areas, such as New York City's Bryant Park and Lincoln Center, now offer light metal chairs to their patrons and allow them to arrange the seating however they want. This is a far cry from the standard anchored benches that we see in many parks and schools.

The urbanist William H. Whyte noted the psychological impact of movable furniture in a park. His groundbreaking 1980 book, *The Social Life of Small Urban Spaces*, launched a mini revolution in the planning of outdoor urban parks. He wrote:

> The possibility of choice is as important as the exercise of it. If you know you can move if you want to, you feel more comfortable staying put.

In other words, if you know you can move a chair, then you will feel better even if you never adjust its location. So, in your garden, make your furniture light and moveable.

Vintage style metal chairs, a perennial favorite, can be moved around easily. They come in many fun colors, as shown here, and add pizazz to the garden.

39. HAVE FUN WITH STONES

The plants are planted, the walks are in. Now what to do in your lovely garden? Well, don't forget the fun you can have by including natural stones into the mix. This resilient, long-lasting material can elicit some imaginative ideas. This is due to stone's unique ability to be many things, from a solitary garden feature to an artful wall to a quiet gravel "sea." And what you create today will weather through the years, forming an enduring companion to the fleeting lives of the flowers and shrubs.

A playful idea is to stack some rounded or flat stones of any size in a tapered pile. The result is a temporary art feature. You can create several of these Zen stone towers, or you can ask your visitors to join in and have a hand in balancing the stones as well. It's a fun game that is certain to engage everyone's power of concentration.

You can go one step beyond and make a tower of stone, sometimes called a cairn. These artful features add a special quality to a garden and can vary widely in appearance. It's best to use flat stones because they stack more easily than round ones. After a while, you may find yourself becoming obsessed with rock stacking!

John Hackenburg creates creative stone towers in his garden with stones he collects from his property. These fun, natural stone creations have become quite elaborate and always bring a smile.

40. GARDEN MAKING ADVICE FROM A ZEN MASTER

What we need today are gardens that can reach deep into people's hearts. —Shunmyo Masuno

Your garden is your personal outdoor world that you co-create with nature. It reflects your wonder and joy of working with plants, stone, and water. Your garden can also be a great way to "reach into people's hearts" as Zen Buddhist monk Shunmyo Masuno has noted. He is a member of the Kenkoh-ji Temple, a monastery in Japan, and is a well-known contemporary garden designer. In addition, Masuno is a professor at Tama Art University and president of a design firm that has completed numerous landscape projects in Japan and overseas. He is a *Shidate-so*, which is defined as a Zen priest who expresses himself through the art of landscape gardening, with great importance given to rock placement. Masuno sees garden making as an intensely personal exercise and gives this sage advice:

There is a Zen proverb that says if a poisonous snake drinks water, it is changed to poison. If a cow drinks water, it is changed to milk. That means that it is up to me whether the same water I drink is changed into poison or into milk. If my heart is not addressed, I can't just create beautiful gardens full of spirituality. Therefore, such gardens are also a mirror of myself. They are myself.

A statue by my front door reminds me of Shunmyo Masuno's advice.

2.

WALLS, PATIOS, WALKS, *and* STEPS

Walls, patios, walks, and steps form the permanent framework of a landscape. They are the functional parts of a garden and tell us where to gather, where to walk, and even how fast to move. For example, a front door landing is a transition space between inside and outside the house. You can make this important area quite welcoming if you create an area that invites people to gather comfortably. Just don't forget to leave space for planters full of flowers for some colorful seasonal flair.

Paved walks offer a wonderful opportunity to display stone, brick, or concrete paving to its best advantage. With a variety of materials to choose from, you can use the one that complements your home and withstands the local climate. The clean lines of smooth concrete are suitable for a modern home. Tawny-colored sandstone matches a desert home, whereas brick pavers add character to a colonial style house. Choose paving that fits its function. For front walks where traffic is high, smooth surfaces are best. A simple stepping-stone path is better suited for gardens or backyards.

By using some of the tips I suggest, you can influence how people move through your garden. You can induce them to walk faster if you provide a walk that is straight and narrow, is paved, and is well lit. A notable and visible destination at the end of the walk will act as a draw and get people to move even quicker. This section shares hardscape tips and includes ideas about paving patterns, types of edging, rounded steps, and much more. As they say, it's all in the details.

41. HOW BIG A PATIO DO YOU NEED?

Do not make your patio too small! Bigger really is better. Some people do not realize how important size consideration is until it is too late. Before you install a patio, make sure to think of all the ways you might use it. Make it larger than an area for just a few chairs because, maybe in the future, you will want a fire pit, an outdoor heater, or lots of decorative pots with flowers.

A key factor to consider is the dimensions of the outdoor furniture you have or plan to buy. The material or style is not an issue, you simply need to know the general shape and size. For example, if you like to eat outside, consider whether you prefer a table that is oval, rectangular, or round. The size and shape of this table may affect the optimal shape of the patio.

You can get the dimensions of the furniture you like from catalogs. They specify the sizes and may show diagrams. You can follow this rule of thumb: a 48-inch-diameter round table with four chairs needs a 12-foot square area; and a 60-inch-diameter round table and six chairs needs a 14-foot square. Don't forget to add space around the perimeter so that people can move around easily.

A useful tip: use blue painter's tape to mark out the overall dimensions of your outdoor furniture. Ideally, you should do this before you buy anything for the patio.

Above: *The rustic fieldstone steps here transformed a steep hillside into a lovely ascent. The 'Limelight' hydrangea* (Hydrangea paniculata grandiflora *'Limelight'*) *at the top of the steps is a floriferous accent in late summer.*

Right: *These long grass steps invite you up a fairly steep hill. Tip: the longer the steps, the less daunting the slope appears.*

42. MAKE THE STEPS THE SHOW

You can make a relatively boring lawn into something special with the addition of just a few long steps. They act as a focal point and set a mood. In other words, steps in a garden steal the show. No matter their appearance, your eye cannot help but follow the steps up or down. They compel you to follow their lead.

Garden steps make any sloped landscape more accessible and inviting. Stone is a natural choice for landscape steps—it is durable, weatherproof, long-lasting, and adds a timeless appearance. But there are many more choices including brick, concrete, and even grass.

I like to install long steps if I can. The longer they are, the more inviting they appear. In one garden, I installed three long grass steps in a slightly sloping lawn. The step risers are fashioned from fieldstone and the treads are lawn. The steps add structure or "bones" to the garden and graciously separate the lower area from the higher one. This is just one example of how a few steps can add magic to a landscape. There is a wealth of design options and materials you can choose from.

Bluestone steps with a chiseled rockface add a rough quality to this hillside. I used native rocks to border these steps. They add to the rough-hewn feeling.

Walls, Patios, Walks, and Steps

43. THE 3, 4, 5 RULE FOR 90-DEGREE CORNERS

When laying out a plant bed, terrace, or fence line, make sure the angles are accurate. This is especially true for 90-degree corners, or right angles. You can use a large-size aluminum carpenter's square, but it helps to double check the angle by using the 3, 4, 5 triangle rule.

Let's say you want to make a fence line that is perpendicular to a wall of your house. Put a stake at the beginning point next to the house. We will call this beginning point A. Run a string line out approximately 90 degrees from point A. Now place a stake at 3 feet along that string line. This is point B. Next, measure 4 feet from the beginning point A against the wall of the house, and place a stake. That is point C.

Now measure the distance between B and C. This is the hypoteneuse of the triangle. If your angle of the string line to the house is square, or 90 degrees, the distance will be 5 feet. If it measures more or less than 5 feet, move the stake at point B to make the length of the string line equal 5 feet. Then you know it is a right angle. This works well with multiples of 3, 4, and 5. For example, you can double the lengths to 6, 8, and 10 feet, or more.

With one line measuring 8 feet along the fence and one line measuring 6 feet extending out at 90 degrees from the fence, the angled line between the two ends should measure 10 feet. This is double the 3, 4, 5 rule described above.

Gardentopia

44. A RAISED WALKWAY FOR SOGGY GROUND

There is nothing more uncomfortable than walking on a path filled with puddles. A raised wood walkway is an attractive alternative to a garden path, especially if you have areas that are soggy or experience seasonal wetness. Here are a couple design ideas to help make a raised walkway appear to be more than a utilitarian wood runway:

- Don't elevate it too much—people may not be as nimble as you may think. A few inches high may be enough.

- There should be multiple posts that extend above both sides of the walkway, as shown here, to provide a feeling of security and to add visual interest.

- Plant tall moisture-loving plants such as Louisiana iris around the elevated walk to make the walkway appear as an integral part of the garden.

These walks can be constructed of weather-resistant materials such as long-lasting composite decking. This material looks like wood but doesn't rot.

This raised wood walkway is at Sleepy Cat Farm in Greenwich, Connecticut. It traverses a wetland area and steps up to follow the sloping ground. It transforms what was an unusable wet zone into an area where a visitor can admire a wetland habitat. You can visit this garden through the Garden Conservancy Open Days program.

Above: *Stone edging can be used in a variety of ways to create different effects in a garden setting. This unique stone edging is in the Japanese Garden of the public garden, Huntington Botanical Gardens, in San Marino, California.*

Below: *You can retain a raised bed with stone edging as we did here.*

45. EDGING MAKES THE DIFFERENCE

A slightly raised edge along a walk, plant bed, or patio is similar to a frame around a picture—it defines a space and makes it feel a little more special. Edging also helps to contain the soil and keep it from spilling out.

There are several natural materials you can use as edging. I often use 1½-inch-thick by 10-inch-wide bluestone pavers, set on edge. The paver should be set into the earth at least 6 to 8 inches deep and extend about 2 to 3 inches above ground level. The visible edge of the bluestone can be treated in several ways. You can use a curved bull-nosed edge for a refined effect, or you can use a chiseled rock face edge for a rustic look. I like a thermal edge, which is a textured but still smooth surface.

Other materials that can be used as edging include thin granite pavers, Belgian blocks, concrete pavers, and bricks. All of these are sturdy and handle the bump of a lawn mower well. They come in a variety of colors and thicknesses. You can also use edging that differs in color from the terrace paving to create a notable contrast.

The granite edging sits 2 to 3 inches above the terrace and borders a plant bed filled with hydrangea and 'Titan Icy Pink' annual vinca (Catharanthus roseus) flowers. The edging separates the terrace from the plant bad, allowing for easier maintenance.

46. MEET AND GREET

A front doorway is a place where people often stop and talk. This is the "meet and greet" area where you welcome your guests when they arrive, and then see them off at the end of a visit. The importance of this outdoor gathering spot is often overlooked but, if you have some space outside your door, you might consider creating an inviting place to facilitate meeting and greeting.

You can make a meet and greet area as large as you want, although it should be able to accommodate at least three people. Additionally, you might want to make it big enough to fit one or two planters. This warm touch allows you to have a seasonal display and is a visual cue that says welcome. A spacious paved area in front of your door also makes your house appear larger.

The paving should match the style of the house, and the space can be somewhat formal as it is the front greeting area. Benches are especially useful when placed in a meet and greet area. In addition to seating, benches provide a spot where you can set down parcels and bags as you open the door. How convenient!

Top: *This large landing invites people to the front steps and is a nice foreground for the natural rock outcrop. Plantings around it make it an integral part of the setting.*

Bottom: *I enlarged the area in front of this door to make it more inviting. Note the inscribed sunray pattern in the granite millstone in the center.*

47. ROUNDED STEPS

The elegant curve of rounded steps insert a graceful note into the landscape. They are versatile, suited to many garden styles, and can be fashioned from materials such as brick, stone, grass, or concrete.

Gertrude Jekyll, the famed English garden designer and writer (1843–1932), endorsed curved outdoor steps and urged people to make the step treads wide and the risers low "so that they are easy-going." This is an apt phrase for the effect that rounded steps have on the landscape. They are casual and inviting. They do not direct or channel people in one direction but, instead, allow them to fan out into the garden. Rounded steps, especially those constructed with grass treads, create quite a romantic look.

Rounded steps can lead to a curved upper landing. Be careful not to make too many risers, otherwise the effect can be daunting and overwhelm the space. The steps do not have to be perfectly semicircular but can simply bow out in the middle. In fact, avoid making the rounded steps with too tight a radius because it creates a cramped look. The gentler the curve, the better.

These bluestone steps lead down to a gravel parking area. The step treads are a well-defined arc. A path light in the plant bed at the end illuminates them in the evening.

Belgian block step risers make a strong line in these curved grass steps. Each of the steps has a pronounced pitch down to facilitate drainage. This is an important detail for ensuring the grass thrives.

48. PLANKING PATTERN—A MODERN TOUCH

A paved terrace within a modern garden requires a sleek paving pattern. A good solution that adds a high design touch is the pattern known as planking, where stone pavers run in horizontal bands along the length of the terrace. Each band varies in width from the one next to it. For example, the first line of pavers in a row might all measure 18 inches wide. The next band, abutting this row, could all measure 30 inches wide. The following band of pavers may be 24 inches wide. Within each row, the pavers should vary in length but not width. This pattern mimics a wood flooring layout. You can use bluestone, limestone, sandstone, or concrete pavers in a planking pattern.

Bluestone paver planking is shown in these photos. It is important to alternate the joints so that they don't line up from row to row. Also make sure the width of each row of paving is sufficiently different from the preceding row. This little change ensures visual interest and movement.

Planking is a popular pattern, and you can see it outdoors in many contemporary settings. It works well in both residential and public landscapes.

I designed this patio using bluestone pavers in a planking pattern. They run parallel to the house, which makes the space seem more spacious. The widest row consists of 3-foot-wide bluestone pavers, the narrowest row is 1 foot. The pots of red geraniums add a great pop of color to the gray patio.

49. PUNCTUATE WITH A BRICK BORDER

If you are installing a patio, consider inserting a band of a different material that provides a contrast of color, texture, and size to the primary paving. The inclusion of a contrasting material such as brick adds a bit of interest to any paved expanse. One option is to incorporate a row or rows of brick pavers toward the outer edge of bluestone terrace. The number of rows of pavers depends on how wide a band you want. The wider the brick band, the more noticeable it is. Set the bricks in a running bond pattern, which means the bricks are placed end on end. This paving pattern works well as a border.

Contrasting borders or bands help define an outdoor space and add a decorative touch. In addition to brick, consider using Belgian block, concrete pavers, or granite pavers to outline a terrace. They create an unusual but attractive border.

A double brick border in a running bond pattern inserts a new color in the stone paving. In this case, the bricks are mortared. Notice the granite paver edging, set 2 inches above the terrace.

Here I used four rows of brick to surround a patio. The stone pattern that it borders is a random naturalistic layout that contrasts markedly with the brick.

50. CEDAR LOG STEPS

If you have a wooded hillside, cedar log steps may be the perfect addition. Cedar logs are long-lasting and insect resistant. They look especially lovely within a woodland setting, surrounded by a mix of ferns, hellebores, and astilbes.

To install these steps, dig a trench and place the soil on both sides of the step area so that it will appear as if the logs were set into the earth. Set a log into the ground as a foundation. Place a second log on top to serve as the step riser. To keep the logs in place, drill a hole through the center of both, insert a $3\frac{1}{2}$-foot-long metal rebar, and pound it into the earth. Place a length of rebar through each end of the logs and one in the center. Remember to keep the top of the metal rebar flush with the top of the log.

Space the log steps evenly, allowing at least 18 inches for a tread depth. Fill in behind each step with small gravel and firmly compact it. You may pound spikes or posts in front of both ends of each step for extra support. Complete the project by adding mulch on the step treads. When you finish, the steps will look like they have always been there.

Above: *Cedar steps with compacted gravel treads are a rustic way to ascend a hill.*

Left: *These log steps are at the Steinhardt Garden in Mt. Kisco, New York. Log steps do not last forever but cedar is a good choice because it doesn't rot as rapidly as other species. The pine needle mulch provides a softness that is appealing.*

51. ENHANCE THE PUBLIC FACE OF YOUR HOUSE

A front walk and drive constitute the public face of a house and project a visual statement of who you are to the world. So, with that in mind, isn't it smart to spruce up the front landscape of your house a little? It makes more of an impression than you may realize. It is a reflection of you.

If you have a small house, you can make it appear larger by installing a wide front entry walk. A small structure with a spacious front walk looks larger than a medium-sized house with a narrow, cramped entry. To enhance the appeal, add some evergreen plants to flank both sides of the walk and bring in some cool planters. Hang a banner, include some lighting, and paint the front door a jazzy color.

Similarly, a driveway can be transformed from being a strip of pavement to a modified parking area, complete with curbing and unique paving. All this effort is worth it, realtors say, because the enhanced curb appeal you create can increase the value of a house by 10 to 15 percent.

Why not add a bench and planters filled with flowers near your front steps? That is what this homeowner did—how inviting!

52. OUTDOOR STEPS—WIDER AND LOWER

Outdoor step treads should be wider and the risers lower than indoor steps. While an interior step can be 8 inches high and look fine, a riser that high outdoors looks unwelcoming. A comfortable outdoor step should be no less than 5 inches high and no higher than 7 inches. A good height for outdoor step risers is from 5½ to 6½ inches high.

An important consideration in step design is the important riser/ tread relationship. The *tread* is the part you step on and the *riser* is the vertical part of the step. If the riser height is in good proportion to the depth of the tread, then the steps will be comfortable to climb. If they are not in good proportion, they can be awkward to walk on. A rule of thumb for calculating outdoor riser and tread measurements is 2 × riser height + tread depth = 26 to 27 inches. This formula suits the length of the average person's stride.

Using this mathematical rule, a common outdoor step dimension is a 5½-inch-high riser with a 16-inch-wide tread; or a 6-inch-high riser with a 14-inch-wide tread. This is simply a guide that can be modified to meet your specific site conditions.

The bluestone steps shown here have 14-inch-wide treads and 6-inch-high risers. This makes for a comfortable ascent outdoors. The step overhang helps rainwater to run off quickly. In this photo, a louvered light set into the cheek wall illuminates these steps at night. The low-growing, spreading 'Blue Pacific' juniper (Juniperus conferta 'Blue Pacific') drapes over the stone.

Gardentopia

53. CAP THAT WALL

A low, freestanding or retaining stone wall can serve as a seat in your garden. The wall should be mortared, stand no higher than 20 inches high, and be capped with smooth stones for seating comfort. Stone wall caps add a finished look to any wall but, more important, help prevent water from seeping into the wall. Of course, they also make a fine seating option. Here are some considerations for a stone wall cap:

THICKNESS OF CAP—The thickness of the capstones should be in proportion to the height and width of the wall. That said, a capstone should be 1½ inches thick or thicker—a thin stone cap looks like a weak gesture. A taller wall requires a proportionately thicker cap.

CAP OVERHANG—A capstone should overhang a wall 1½ to 2 inches on each side. The overhang directs water to fall straight down.

EDGE TREATMENT—There are a variety of edge finishes to choose from, such as an unfinished saw edge, thermal, bullnose, eased edge, and rock face.

A fieldstone wall with a bluestone cap, as shown here, is an inviting place to sit. Make sure to allow an adequate overhang to ensure that rain will fall directly down into the earth off the edge of the cap.

54. WHY WE LOVE NICHES

How lovely it is to sit in an outdoor niche! In this space, protected on three sides, we are in a world of our own. Our preference for this nestled space must hark back to an instinctive desire for a safe resting place. Like cats in boxes, we enjoy being in a private place where we can take time out from the bustle of life and simply sit, watch, and reflect.

A niche in a garden is intriguing. You can create a three-sided sitting area by building a low wall or planting a hedge. Both elements do a great job of creating a permanent, enclosed area. The height of the wall or hedge does not need to be high—30 inches tall is sufficient. You can also create a temporary niche using tall planters filled with foliage. Line them up as a wall on three sides to make a small outdoor sanctuary.

One word of caution: Do not make the niche too small and constricting. The space should provide enough room for several seats or a bench. Measure the furniture you plan to use and make sure there is sufficient space to fit them all. Remember too that a hedge will grow wider and will need to be pruned.

Above: *This niche, bounded by stacked limestone walls, was made specifically for this classic bench. This is at the Dallas Arboretum and Botanical Garden.*

Left: *Here is a niche that is 15 feet long. It contains the outdoor furniture perfectly. You cannot resist taking a seat in this protected area.*

55. SETTING STEPPING STONES

A stepping stone path is a rustic way to lead people through a garden. A series of irregularly shaped stones set flush with the earth offers a direct relationship with our natural surroundings because we must watch carefully as we step. It forces us to look down at our feet. The arrangement and pattern of the stepping stones also influence how people move through the landscape. You can slow visitors down by setting the stones far apart or by placing them side by side. Here are some tips for setting step stones as a garden path:

- Set the stones in the ground so that they extend above the soil by 2 or 3 inches. These are called "floating stones" in Japan.

- Place the stepping stones in straight lines in varying intervals between them. Or you can offset them for a "left foot, right foot" pace (like the tracks that shore birds leave in the sand). To walk on these stones, you must look down, which serves to make low-growing plants and other ground-level features more noticeable.

- Set a much wider stone across the path every so often to invite people to stop and enjoy a view.

Stepping stones can be set in gravel, as we did here. It looks lovely when autumn leaves add a bit of color.

Surround natural stepping stones with fine mulch for a soft woodland feel.

56. MAKE MINE HERRINGBONE

A brick patio conveys a homey, familiar feeling, especially when it is surrounded by greenery. Brick can withstand wear and tear, and it comes in a variety of colors. You can even use reclaimed brick to give a landscape a historic, well-crafted look. But a large area of brick paving can appear harsh and monolithic if there is nothing to break the expanse. This is why the paving pattern that you use is so important.

One of the options is to set brick pavers in a distinctive zigzag or herringbone pattern. The diagonal lines of the brick create visual movement. This design can be subtly enhanced if you alternate the colors of the brick. I use this pattern in my landscapes for its dynamic appearance.

The space between the bricks may be filled with mortar, if you choose. Brick paving that is not mortared has a more informal look. A "soldier course" of brick can be used as an outer border to contain the patio. This course is a row of brick that runs perpendicular to the primary herringbone pattern, and it provides a neat finish to the overall paved area.

Above: *Here a large expanse of mortared herringbone brick is divided with strips of bluestone. Note the soldier course of brick at the perimeter.*

Left: *A wide band of irrigated lawn or artificial turf acts as a soft "rest" for the eyes. Make the band at least 12 inches wide, preferably more. Trim with a string trimmer.*

57. A CONNOISSEUR OF STONE WALLS

Something there is that doesn't love a wall . . .
—Robert Frost

Stone walls are the anchors of a garden. They speak to us of endurance. They define our property boundaries and retain our hillsides. They are a true collaboration between man and nature.

Have you ever admired a natural stone wall? It is a visual celebration of nature's most durable material and can be so interesting. Some walls are constructed of small stones such that they appear as a tapestry of stone. Other walls are made from large angular rocks that form a mosaic of rocky faces. Blocklike, rectangular stones form an ordered wall, while weathered, lichen-covered fieldstone, with moss and ferns rooted in the crevices, create a wall of the softest kind. There are so many kinds of stone walls to admire.

Once you start to notice the differences in stone walls, you may, like me, see them as artworks in their own right. As I look at a particular wall, I silently applaud the stone mason who built it and the craftsmanship that went into it. I have become what I call a connoisseur of stone walls and I appreciate them wherever I go. Won't you join me?

The appearance of stone walls varies with the kind of stone used and how it was built. The possibilities are almost endless.

3.

THEME GARDENS

*The garden should fit its owner or his or her tastes,
just as one's clothes do; it should be neither too
large nor too small, but just comfortable.*

—Gertrude Jekyll

Theme gardens revolve around a unifying idea or type of plant. They highlight our interests and are fun to create. As Gertrude Jekyll, a British horticulturist, garden designer, and writer, noted, a garden should fit our taste. Themes such as butterfly gardens have become quite popular, and some even feature ornaments and accents that fit the narrative. Native plant gardens and rain gardens are also popular themes. Many theme gardens are designed to benefit the environment; what better reason is there than this to have a theme garden? But there are other themes to consider. An herbal tea garden is perfect for a tea drinker. Such a garden could feature chamomile, lemon verbena, and mint among an assortment of aromatic herbs. A small table and chair could be added for afternoon tea in the garden. How enchanting!

Your garden theme can be a personal one. For example, you can show off your collection of antique statuary or your favorite color. You can even design your outdoor space for a particular time of day. For example, if you get home from work late in the day, why not create a luminous "evening garden" where white flowers and silvery foliage plants reflect the moonlight? Or if you loved your vacation in Hawaii, a tropical splash garden may be an alluring theme for you.

This section offers a variety of theme ideas for your garden. You can focus on a type of plant, a color, or even an artist. A theme requires that you follow its limitations. For example, a native plant garden in New England cannot sport exotic plants from the Canary Islands. A ferny garden should consist mostly of ferns. These restrictions provide a clear sense of unity or purpose and can elevate your garden so that it becomes something special.

If you like the idea of a theme garden but don't know which theme to choose, consider what you enjoy. You may love the look of succulents or the scent of fragrant flowers. Best of all, theme gardens appeal to kids. So why not try a sunflower garden or a blue garden? You can get the children out of the house and introduce them to gardening at the same time.

Page 122: *This stone cupid is surrounded by the white flowers and bold foliage of oakleaf hydrangeas (*Hydrangea quercifolia*).*

58. CUPID'S GARDEN

A garden without its statue is like a sentence without its verb.
—Joseph W. Beach

In the seventeenth century, Mr. Abraham Cuper, a gardener by trade, established a public tea garden on the River Thames in London. It became known as Cupid's Garden, which sounded similar to his name. The romantic tea garden captured the public's imagination. People flocked to Cupid's Garden, and it grew in size and popularity.

Today a cupid's garden revolves around the theme of love and courtship. A statue of a cherub, with his golden arrows of love, is certainly appropriate here. The statue can be located in a central part of the space and then be surrounded with sumptuous, fragrant flowers in profusion. A small Victorian fountain would fit in as well. Romance permeates the air. If you enjoy the Victorian fascination with the language of flowers and their meanings, you can plant blossoms that speak of love. Here are a few examples of certain flowers and what each symbolizes:

Forget-me-not—*True Love*   Lilacs—*First Emotions of Love*

Violet—*Faithful Love*   Red Rose—*Love*

Tulips—*Declaration of Love*   Rose of Sharon—*Consumed by Love*

In the language of flowers, pale pink roses convey grace and joy. They are perfect for a Cupid's garden.

59. REMEMBER THE POLLINATORS

The sole task of flowers, with their color, fragrance, and form, is to be pollinated by butterflies, bees, insects, bats, or birds. Without flowers—and their pollinators—we would not have any seeds or fruit! Sadly, global evidence suggests that our pollinator populations are declining rapidly. This is due to pesticide use and habitat destruction. What can we do to bring back the pollinators?

If you have a sunny open spot, some shelter from wind, and can provide fresh water, then you have an opportunity to create a pollinator haven. If you want to attract butterflies, place a few rocks or a patch of gravel in the path of the morning sun. This is an ideal spot where butterflies, who need to warm up to move, can enjoy a morning bask before heading out to seek nectar.

Plant nectar-rich plants and choose colors that a given pollinator likes. For example, hummingbirds are particularly fond of red, while bees seem to prefer flowers in the purple/violet range. The Xerces Society (www.xerces.org) has lists of pollinator-friendly plants for regions in the United States and abroad.

Clockwise: *Bees and butterflies love clustered mountain mint* (Pycnanthemum muticum*). It has pinkish-white, aromatic flowers. Blooms August through September.*

The 'Torch' Mexican sunflower (Tithonia rotundifolia 'Torch'*) is a vivid-colored cultivar for attracting monarch butterflies. It is a tall plant with a long bloom period. Plants thrive in summer heat.*

The shade-loving bottlebrush buckeye (Aesculus parviflora*) is a striking shrub that attracts masses of butterflies. The upright cylindrical spikes of feathery white flowers appear in June and July in a picturesque candelabra-like branching habit.*

'Lucky White' lantana is a great butterfly flower. Other summer pollinator magnets include ageratum, sedum, dahlias, and cosmos.

60. A STROLL GARDEN

Walking inspires and promotes conversation that is grounded in
the body, and so it gives the soul a place where it can thrive.
—Thomas Moore, *Soul Mates*

The art of strolling can be rediscovered in a garden. A stroll garden harks back to a slower time when people would saunter through a landscape, admiring its treasures and enjoying the time to converse. Wide paths with notable scenes or plants to look at are suggested for such a garden. Traditional Japanese stroll gardens placed great importance on offering different views and interesting features along a curving walk. The goal was to provide a garden where one could be refreshed and enjoy a sense of discovery, no matter how small the space. If you provide a loop path for strolling, plant something interesting to look at and perhaps offer a change in light and shade.

A walkway in a stroll garden should be made wider than normal. This will promote a slower pace and allow visitors to amble side by side. Gentle slopes, rather than steep hills, are the rule here. Slightly curved paths are preferred over straight ones. The aim is to have the garden reveal itself in stages, hiding and offering up its delights in turn. This is the beauty of stroll gardens: to provide visitors a journey in nature.

Left: *The selection of paving for a garden path determines how fast a person moves through a garden. Here the smooth surfaced path in Descanso Gardens in La Cañada Flintridge, California, allows visitors to walk freely.*

Right: *A grassed walk leads past curving plant beds in this garden designed for strolling.*

61. A ROCK CREVICE GARDEN

A rock outcrop with deep fissures and cracks is a perfect venue for a crevice garden. Plants tucked in narrow rocky openings create a soft contrast to the stone around them. With a little care and gentle watering, you can make it a true rock garden.

To start, fill each small crack with a little bit of soil mix (topsoil, peat moss, lime, and fertilizer). Lodge in a pebble to hold the soil pocket in place and then plant tough, low-growing plants. Note that if the plants prefer specific, dry conditions, then you should add some small stone grit to the soil mix.

Use small plants (plants that fit in small pots that are about 3 inches diameter) that will fit in the crevices. Remove the plant from the container and gently spread out its roots before inserting it in the soil pocket. Make sure to water it in, and then keep it moist as it gets acclimated.

For added pizazz, add some drought-tolerant annual flowers such as the blue Swan River daisy (*Brachycome iberidifolia*) or yellow Dahlberg daisy (*Thymophylla tenuiloba*) in selected crevices. The long blooming flowers will cloak the rock outcrop in color all summer.

Top, left: *These lady ferns thrive in shady crevices and will spread if left alone.*

Top, right: *The native bloodroot (*Sanguinaria canadensis*) likes to grow in a rocky crevice. Its unique leaves unfurl into large, waterlily-like foliage. Grows in partial shade.*

Bottom: *Candytuft (*Iberis sempervirens*) is a spring flowering perennial that is a favorite in crevice gardens because of its drought tolerance.*

62. MORE KITCHEN GARDENS, PLEASE

A kitchen garden is more than a fenced-in vegetable plot—it is also quite lovely to look at. Normally located close to the house, a traditional kitchen garden, also known as a potager, incorporates vegetables, herbs, and perennial and annual flowers in an elegant yet productive garden layout. The crops may be special or heirloom varieties, ordered early from a seed catalog.

The design of a kitchen garden is normally a classic, rectilinear layout and may have additions such as upright *tuteurs*, pots, or a bench. The perimeter fence and gate, used to keep critters out, can be quite decorative. It may also have a wall to shelter one or more sides. Many kitchen gardens have raised beds. This helps the soil warm up earlier in cooler climates and ensures that the soil drains well. Raised beds also make it easier to harvest low-growing salad crops.

An important consideration for a kitchen garden is the amount of sun the garden will receive. The best location will get at least seven hours of full sun a day, preferably starting in the morning. A kitchen garden does not have to be large, because it can produce quite a bit if well tended.

A kitchen garden favorite—the vivid, edible flowers of Nasturtium 'Alaska Mix.' Great for a kid's vegeatble garden as it has big seeds and tolerates poor soil and heat or cold.

The blue/green foliage of Brussels sprouts.

'Ruby Red' Swiss chard is both beautiful and nutritious.

A strong fence is essential! The rows here are kept neat by bluestone edging and fresh layers of mulch.

Clockwise: 'Little Lamb' Hydrangea (Hydrangea paniculata 'Little Lamb') makes a spectacular mass planting at the Berkshire Botanical Garden in Massachusetts. The other three photos illustrate the range of colors and flower shapes that hydrangeas provide.

63. HYDRANGEA MADNESS

Hydrangeas, with their large pink, white, or purple/blue blooms, are mesmerizing in the garden. They add a lushness that nothing else can match. They are easy to care for, and you have many varieties to choose from! Maybe that is why hydrangeas are one of the most popular flowering shrubs.

You can have a summer garden overflowing with hydrangeas of all kinds. Dwarf hydrangeas, such as the white blooming *Hydrangea paniculata* Bobo®, grows just 30 to 36 inches tall. These are perfect for planting in containers. You can train the tall-growing 'Limelight' panicled hydrangea (*Hydrangea paniculata* 'Limelight') as a small tree. There are even climbing hydrangeas (*Hydrangea anomala* subsp. *petiolaris*) that adhere to a wall. And the flowers, both fresh and dried, make stunning floral arrangements. Hydrangea madness indeed.

For summer privacy, plant a hedge of blue mophead hydrangea (*Hydrangea macrophylla*) or the taller panicled hydrangea. These deciduous shrubs lose their leaves in fall so they will not screen well in the winter.

The unique quality of some hydrangeas is their ability to change flower color depending on the acidity of the soil. While panicled hydrangeas are white that changes to pink, mopheads and lacecap hydrangeas respond to acidic soil to yield blue or lavender hydrangea blooms. They turn a pinkish hue in alkaline soil.

Endless Summer® 'Twist-n-Shout' lacecap hydrangea blooms from early summer to early fall. The flowers are excellent for cutting. The leaves turn an outstanding burgundy in the fall. Photo by Laura McKillop.

64. WHIMSY? WHY NOT?

Whimsy is the word we use for playful and amusing items. They are not meant to be serious. Whimsical garden features are touches of fun that lighten up an outdoor space. They can be colorful and somewhat silly. They may not be high art, but who cares? The idea is to say it with a smile. And where else but in a garden should we relax and just enjoy some levity?

Whimsical items in a landscape are normally small accents placed in out-of-the-way spaces that wait to be discovered. But they do not necessarily have to be small or hidden. I had a client who placed a 7-foot-tall fiberglass statue of a polka-dotted elephant, standing on one foot, right next to the swimming pool I had designed for them. Big time whimsy, for sure.

A simple addition of a tin can man or a teapot fountain can turn your garden into a place of enchantment. A small frog with a crown will turn heads. The gnome and adorable animal statues may add fun to your garden but be careful, it can become an obsession. They proliferate easily.

Left: *A crown prince frog sits atop a golden globe reigning over white angelonia, 'Blue Hawaii' ageratum, and white petunias.*

Below: *This bench is in Luna Parc in Montague, New Jersey. It is a temple to whimsy. You can visit this unique house and grounds on special open days and pick up some great whimsical ideas for indoors and out. Check out their website: www.lunaparc.com.*

Left: *White chrysanthemums planted in a stately planter brighten up a dark corner in the moonlight.*

Below: *I planted a large grouping of Japanese dappled willow (Salix integra 'Hakuro-nishiki') on a hillside. These shine in the evening due to its green and white foliage. This fast-growing, adaptable shrub requires constant pruning to keep it in this mounded shape.*

65. INTO THE MOONLIGHT

"Moon gardens" extend our enjoyment of the outdoors into the evening. These landscapes, filled with white, silver, and gray plants, are meant to reflect the moon's luminous glow when it is near full and washes us with heavenly lunar light. These landscapes are particularly lovely when the moon is full on a warm summer evening. The white foliage and flowers can create an almost mystical setting.

To enhance the sparkle of a moon garden, consider adding silvery-gray foliage plants such as dusty miller (*Senecio cineraria*), lamb's ears (*Stachys byzantina*), and curry plant (*Helichrysum italicum*). White benches also help. For a shady garden, try white-leaved plants such as 'White Feather' hosta, 'White Christmas' caladiums, or white 'Okina' lilyturf (*Liriope muscari* 'Okina'). Stringing some small lights in the trees adds to the magic. Even light-colored lichen on rocks shines on a moonlit night. Eye-popping.

If you want an elaborate moon garden, build a moon-viewing platform just like the Japanese and Chinese gardeners did in the past. After the day is done, you can sit on the platform with a cup of tea, facing the moon, surrounded by night-blooming flowers, and bask in the moonlight.

*Huge blooms of white 'Casa Blanca' oriental lilies (*Lilium 'Casa Blanca'*), planted in a mass, will envelop you with perfume on a warm moonlit evening.*

66. FOOD FOR THE NOSE

Aroma is food for the nose. An average person draws 23,000 breaths a day, and the scents contained in each breath convey information and provoke memories in a way that nothing else can. The effect of a scent is immediate because our sense of smell is connected directly to the limbic section (emotional responses) of the brain. It's no wonder that scent can control stress levels, heart rate, and even blood pressure! For this reason, you may want to create a fragrant garden where you can enjoy both the sight and scent of your surroundings. Here are three tips for using scented plants in a landscape:

- Place fragrant plants by a door so you can catch a whiff of the aroma as you enter. Try a 'Jasmine' Tobacco or Nicotiana (*Nicotiana alata*). Its white trumpet flowers open at dusk and permeate the air with a jasmine scent.

- Heat encourages plants to release their scent. Place scented plants on a sunny patio or near a south-facing wall. The reflected heat may make the odors a little stronger.

- Place fragrant plants in an enclosed space such as a walled garden or small side yard. The scent will collect here, and not be carried away by the breeze, to surround you with aroma as you sit outside.

Heliotrope (Heliotropium aborescens) is a flowering annual known for its vanilla scent. The variety, 'Fragrant Delight,' has dark purple flowers and grows in a mounded habit. Plant in a large container to bring its cherry-pie scent closer to the nose.

'Scentsation' honeysuckle (Lonicera periclymenum 'Scentsation') is a showy vine with extremely fragrant yellow flowers. This honeysuckle has a long bloom time and can be trained up a trellis or fence.

Above: *The entry to the Lerner Garden of the Five Senses is through a "larch arch" where the boughs of two weeping larch trees drape over visitors' heads.*

Below: *The pond in the center of the Lerner Garden at Coastal Maine Botanical Gardens offers visitors a chance to touch and view the flowing water.*

67. A GARDEN OF THE FIVE SENSES

A garden designed to celebrate the five senses—see, hear, touch, smell, and taste—is a "sensational" idea. Why not add items in your garden to appeal to each sense? Plant lilacs and summersweet (*Clethra alnifolia*) for scent, place rocks for touch, and add splashing water for sound. You can also plant edible nasturtium flowers for taste! For some fun ideas, look to the beautiful Coastal Maine Botanical Gardens in Boothbay, Maine. One of their special gardens is the inventive Lerner Garden of the Five Senses.

The ¾-acre Lerner Garden has five separate zones to represent each sense. Its features are accessible to all visitors. A pond and pavilion form the heart of the garden where soothing sound is provided by trickling cascades and a waterwall. A labyrinth of raised, smooth river stones set in the ground offers a chance to walk with bare feet on a textured surface. There are fuzzy lamb's ears leaves to touch, herbal thyme to sniff, granite rocks to sit on, and vegetables to taste. And there is much more, such as striker stones, which border the main paths to assist the visually disabled. Add Coastal Maine Botanical Gardens to your list of must-visit gardens.

At the Lerner Garden, you can find a vertical cubical stone with recessed holes cut into one side. It is called a "sound stone." Place your head inside a hole and hum or sing to experience the resonant sound of stone.

68. CELEBRATE THE ROCKS

Any large, solitary rocks in your garden should not be overlooked. They are potential features of interest and can make a great theme. In other words, if you have large or unmovable rocks on your property, why not show off their enduring qualities? Unearth them, expose them, and wash them off with a strong jet of water from a garden hose. They can be the basis for a rock garden.

One of my favorite things to do is to reveal a hidden rock outcrop or boulder. It is like digging for treasure. You can use a small masonry brush to sweep off debris from rocks in the garden. You can place more rocks around them and also plant a green leafy plant or a fleshy low-growing sedum next to them. The contrast of the hard rock and soft leaves or flowers provides a visual counterpoint in a garden.

Rocks can be interesting all by themselves, but a rock garden featuring many different types of plants is a wonderful theme. In a rocky woodland area plant ferns, Hellebores, Epimediums, and dwarf iris amongst the stones. If your rock garden is out in the sun, highlight it with some heat-loving flowers like gomphrena (*Gomphrena globosa*) or tickseed (*Coreopsis*). You do not have to put many plants next to a rock—just enough to call attention to it. You could say the theme of your garden is Rock On.

Above: *Unusual rocks at the Dallas Arboretum and Botanical Garden in Texas were placed there for their uncommon, punctuated appearance.*

Left: *The combination of hard rock and soft plants always catches the eye. Here New Guinea impatiens and 'Evergold' sedge (Carex hachijoensis 'Evergold') contrast with a moss-covered stone.*

Top, left: *The red berries of the prolific scarlet firethorn* (Pyracantha coccinea) *attract the beautiful cedar waxwing. These colorful, sociable birds are voracious eaters and it is believed that their red wingtips derive from their diet of berries.*

Top, right: *Crabapples are small-statured ornamental trees known for their fruit. The varieties that have persistent small "crabapples," less than ¾ inch in diameter, can feed birds into the winter. Some bird-friendly cultivars include 'Sargent,' 'Red Splendor,' and 'Donald Wyman.'*

Left: *Multicolored coleus complement the red berries of the doublefile viburnum* (Viburnum plicatum tomentosum *'Mariesii'*) *in late summer. The berries of this viburnum are held above the leaves, making them visible. Birds have excellent color vision, which may explain the prevalence of red among edible berries.*

69. BIRDSCAPING WITH BERRIED PLANTS

Berries of our native plants are not only pretty to view but also necessary for our feathered friends. You can attract a host of hungry birds to your garden in late summer and fall with the fruit of dogwoods (*Cornus*), crabapples (*Malus*), elderberries (*Sambucus*), and viburnum. These provide essential energy for birds as they make their long migrations to more southern climes. You may see birds such as robins, bluebirds, thrushes, catbirds, cardinals, finches, and waxwings taking up a brief and satisfying residence in your backyard. Berryscaping is the way to go when you want a birdscape theme.

Chokeberry (*Aronia arbutifolia*) is a native berried plant that holds on to its red fruit over the winter. This wetland shrub, true to its name, has fruits that are quite bitter. But because the berries persist all winter they feed the birds that remain up north. The 'Viking' black chokeberry (*Aronia melanocarpa* 'Viking') has extra-large black berries that are less astringent. These berries also stay through the winter, feeding the first returning robins in the spring. Viking is also valued for its ability to self-pollinate. The leaves turn orange and burgundy in the fall and form a spectacular contrast to the dark purple berries.

70. MEDICINAL GARDEN, ANYONE?

Plants are our original medicine cabinet. Some garden plants, especially herbs, are still commonly grown to treat ailments. Plants with medicinal properties are perfect for a garden with a healing theme. Lemon balm (*Melissa officinalis*) is an herb well worth growing—its leaves have been used as far back as the Middle Ages to make a tea that helps reduce anxiety and promote sleep. Lemon balm is a member of the mint family, and its leaves impart a lovely lemony taste. Great for stress relief! Another helpful herb is feverfew (*Tanacetum parthenium*). Its daisylike flowers are quite lovely and a tea made from the leaves may be effective in the treatment of some migraine headaches.

Peppermint has long been used as a medicinal herb. Tea made from peppermint leaves calms stomach upsets. It is a good idea to grow peppermint in a pot (you can set it in the earth) because its roots spread so easily. In colonial America, dried leaves of butterfly weed (*Asclepias tuberosa*) were made into a tea to treat chest inflammations, thus giving butterfly weed an alternative name: pleurisy root.

Another wonderful plant to grow in a pot or in a garden is the succulent aloe vera. This plant's fleshy leaves, when cut, exude a soothing gel that is an effective salve for treating burns.

Clockwise: *Why not add a small painted sign denoting the theme of your garden? Make the letters large enough to read from a distance.*

Holy Basil or Tulsi *is an aromatic cousin of our common basil. It is native to India where it is planted in a home as a sign of welcome. Its leaves and flowers are used as a medicinal tea for colds, coughs, and mental clarity.*

*Purple coneflower (*Echinacea*) is easy to grow and withstands drought. Its daisylike flower and its roots can be made into an immune-boosting tea or tincture.*

*Feverfew (*Tanacetum parthenium*) is an herb with small white and yellow flowers that bloom from June through August. It grows well in sun or shade and is drought tolerant.*

Variegated 'Pretoria' canna lily (Canna 'Pretoria') has orange flowers and light glossy green leaves striped with bands of white, cream, and yellow. I planted them here in a large group.

71. TROPICAL SPLASH

A vision of paradise can come a little closer to home if you have what I call a tropical splash garden in your backyard. So get out the tiki torches, string the overhead lights, and add semi-hardy plants with lush foliage to your surroundings.

Tropical-inspired gardens rely on plants known as "temperennials" to create the mood. These are plants that are hardy in warmer parts of the country but in the north must be overwintered indoors. The term was coined by Pierre Bennerup of Sunny Border Nurseries to describe a great number of plants that are used as annuals in the colder climates. Many of them, like elephant's ears (*Colocasia esculenta*) and giant dracaena (*Cordyline australis* 'Purple Tower'), sport exotic leaves and colors.

An easy-to-grow tropical-looking plant is the colorful canna lily (*Canna*). These lilies have large leaves and tall, colorful flowers. For a real centerpiece, plant elephant ears. The 'Thailand Giant' elephant ears (*Colocasia gigantea* 'Thailand Giant') has green leaves up to 5 feet long by 4 feet wide each! And, of course, don't forget caladiums, hostas, and gardenias when creating a tropical heaven outside your door.

Got a slightly wet spot? Then try ornamental rhubarb (Rheum palmatum 'Atrosanguineum'), a perennial with very large dark green leaves with red undersides. It typically grows to a 6- to 10-inch leafy mound.

72. FERNY WOODLAND

Ferns, with their delicate green fronds, add luxuriant texture to a shady garden, especially when planted in large groups. They make a quiet, shadowy area come alive. These are ancient plants, and some types of ferns, like cinnamon fern (*Osmunda cinnamomea*), have been around since the dinosaur era! No wonder they lend an almost prehistoric air when grown in profusion along a walk, in a wooded area, or in a quiet corner.

The variety of fern species to choose from are tremendous. They vary in size, leaf type, color, and growth habit. You can plant low-growing ferns like the Japanese painted fern around rocks or a stone wall. You can border a woodland path with tall, stately ferns like the hardy 'Ghost' fern (*Athyrium* 'Ghost'), or you can plant delicate ferns like the Northern Maidenhair fern (*Adiantum pedatum*) to peek through other plants. For a welcoming statement by a front door, plant some upright tropical ferns like 'Kimberly Queen' Australian sword ferns (*Nephrolepis obliterata* 'Kimberly Queen") in a tall planter. Ferns can be mixed with other shade lovers beneath trees or on the north side of a house. For example, in such settings I like to mix 'Fortune's Holly' fern (*Cyrtomium fortunei*) with the evergreen Christmas fern (*Polystichum acrostichoides*) and the blue-flowering evergreen groundcover 'Bowles' myrtle (*Vinca minor* 'Bowles').

Top, left: *An urn filled with ferns sits atop a raised stone base. More ferns line a shady gravel walk in this private garden.*

Top, right: *Ostrich fern (*Matteuccia struthiopteris*) is a native growing in zones 3–9. It is a tall fern with graceful, featherlike fronds. Easy to grow and deer resistant!*

Bottom: *The native bracken fern (*Pteridium aquilinum*) typically grows to 3 feet tall and 4 feet wide in dry woodlands. Coarse, divided fronds rise tilt to being almost horizontal. Each frond can be 3 feet long.*

The silvery white, serrated foliage of Artemisia 'Silver Brocade' combines beautifully with the dainty blue flowers of the long blooming Laurentia 'Blue Star' (Laurentia axillaris 'Blue Star') and white-fringed 'Telstar Picotee' dianthus.

73. A COTTAGE GARDEN

Everyone loves a cottage garden, with its exuberant medley of colorful flowers that weave around each other. It is a free-flowing scene with flowering plants cascading over paths and vines climbing walls. Cottage gardens are perfect for small spaces, front yards, and anywhere where a welcoming casual flower garden is suitable. Other garden elements that fit the cottage garden theme are the classic picket fence and gate, clipped hedges to contain sprawling flowers, or a lattice trellis or freestanding *tuteur*, a traditional French structural support, usually pyramidal, used to train plants to grow vertically.

The backbone of a cottage garden is tall, flowering plants such as delphinium, garden phlox, climbing roses, or hydrangeas. Add vines such as honeysuckle or clematis and you have the makings of a delightful garden! The plant beds can be extra wide to contain all these marvelous plants, and adding a small stepping stone path through them will help make maintenance tasks easier.

Edge the beds with lady's mantle, bergenia, bleeding heart, coral bells, or dianthus. Plant some mid-height allium, yarrow, and tulips behind them. Your cottage garden will brighten anyone's cloudy day.

The mix of flowers flowing over a walk create a cottage garden scene. Having an evergreen backdrop makes the floral display more effective.

74. A GARDEN FOR A SMALL SPACE

If you have a small space and want a garden, the answer may be cascading greenery. Hanging plants, vines trained on railings, and narrow planters packed with small succulents and annuals offer ways to create a compact landscape on your balcony, deck, or raised terrace. There are many options:

- Train a vining plant such as Dutchman's pipe (*Aristolochia macrophylla*) along a stair or balcony railing. Or let 'Goldflame' honeysuckle (*Lonicera x heckrottii* 'Goldflame') twirl around a lattice screen. I have a climbing hydrangea on a homemade screen and it forms a narrow, blooming verdant divider.

- Make an upright screen from pegboard. Vary the size of hooks that fit into the pegs and then mount small containers of hanging plants. By using different protruding lengths of hangers and varying the sizes of the planters and types of plants, you will create a unique green wall.

- Attach hanging planters from overhead hooks. Using straps of different lengths, hang various plants at different heights. The look is like an overhead chandelier of green.

- Buy some clear, round planters and insert air plants. These lightweight hanging planters can be used anywhere.

- Make the most of window boxes. Grow both upright and hanging plants in them.

This succulent plant, a hybrid between species of Grap-topetalum and sedum, shows off pendulous gray/green rosettes in a repurposed, antique baptismal font. The plant is frost tender but can be wintered indoors if kept dry. This is Lotusland in Montecito, California.

Dutchman's pipe (Aristolochia macrophylla) is a deciduous, climbing vine that is an old-fashioned favorite grown for its large, heart-shaped, overlapping leaves. It can quickly cover a screen or railing with attractive, deep green foliage.

Ricky Boscarino creates art from virtually anything. Blue bowling balls populate a fern bed at his art-filled home, Luna Parc, in Sussex County, New Jersey. Visit his website to see his open house days: www.lunaparc.com.

Do you collect pine cones? Make a mound of them as a feature in your garden. Here the impressive pine cones of the Coulter pine are piled up to create an eye-catching element. Everyday art, for sure.

75. EVERYDAY "ART" IN THE GARDEN

It is the point of view that sanctifies; it is selection and placement that will make anything a sculpture, even an old shoe. —Isamu Noguchi

Looking at items with new eyes can make anything artful. If you see the world this way, then old bottles, polished tree roots, or even a watering can will serve as an art object. Who says that Uncle Fred's old wheelbarrow, sitting among colorful cosmos and oxeye daisies, is not a sculpture?

So go ahead and use an everyday item as an art object in your garden. You can highlight anything that catches your fancy, even a collection of bowling balls. In this approach, art is in the eye of the beholder, and you do not have to be limited to what others may say is art. If it lifts your spirits and delights you, then you can say that it is art.

As Isamu Noguchi, the Japanese American sculptor and designer, said, "It is the point of view that sanctifies."

Tree roots were cleaned and polished to become a work of art at Phyllis Warden's garden in Bedford, New York. You can see this during the Open Days held by Garden Conservancy.

4.

COLOR
in the
GARDEN

*Color is all. When color is right, form is right.
Color is everything, color is vibration like music;
everything is vibration.*

—Marc Chagall

Nothing affects us as strongly as color in a garden. It is the first thing we notice when we enter a space. Yellow catches the eye, blue revitalizes, and green soothes. As artist Marc Chagall noted, these sensations are based on the vibration or light frequency of the color. Once you know this, you can use color in a landscape to set a mood. For example, color experts say that houses will sell faster with yellow flower borders in front. Maybe this is because yellow is the happy color and attracts our attention. Similarly, red plants or red features add an energetic punch to any scene. A small dash of red brightens up a plant bed or a shrub border.

The most restful color is green, in all its many shades and tones. No wonder nature chose to surround us with this nourishing color. The frequency of green is midway on the light spectrum, calming us with its natural balance of cool and warm undertones. Studies have found that a predominantly green setting relaxes our mind. So a garden of green is a therapeutic place to be. Gardentopia, indeed.

Our response to color outdoors is greatly dependent on the quality of available sunlight. The intensity of the sun's rays and the time of year influence our perception of color. For example, in early spring when the light is soft, many people thrill to pastel colors and the thought of bright orange flowers is anathema to them. But as the year progresses, and the sun becomes stronger and higher in the sky, the pastel colors wash out in the summer light and the golds and oranges are glorious.

The effect of light on color holds true for the varying time of day. In the morning the sun's rays are gentle and, for this reason, pastel-colored flowers in east- and north-facing beds look wonderful. The bright, bold colors hold their own in south- and west-facing plant beds when the afternoon sun is at its brightest. It is all about the light.

Color is nature's communication system. It tells insects where the all-important nectar and pollen in flowers is located. It does this through color intensity and patterning. Brightly colored blossoms alert the pollinators that the nectar-laden flower is waiting for them. And patterned blooms, with multicolored petal markings, are similar to bull's-eyes. The bee, butterfly, or hummingbird follows the color patterning to the desired target. Think about this the next time you see the radial color pattern on a flower—it is simply a signaling system!

This captivating topic is a lot fun and, like all discussions about color, subject to personal opinion. I suggest that you be bold and use large expanses of color for the best effect. Plant a mass of yellow roses or blue evergreens. Or mix similar intensity colors together—blend pastels with pastels, bright colors with other bright colors. If you have royal purple iris, mix it with other jewel-toned colors. Or blend dusky dark purples with earth tones such as golden yellow or deep orange. There is so much you can do with color.

The tips in this section revolve around the use of color outdoors. I give suggestions for one-color gardens, playing with color, and colorful plant schemes. I hope this section encourages you to see the colors in your garden with renewed vision. As the great English garden designer Gertrude Jekyll noted, "As for the matter of color, what may be observed is simply without end."

A striking bromeliad (Aechmea blancheti-ana 'Orange') *combines an upright shape and orange color to create an eye-catching plant. In spring, red flower stalks emerge from the center rosette of leaves to add to the display.*

76. TRY SOME YELLOW AND CALL ME IN THE MORNING

Feeling down? Surround yourself with yellow in your garden. Yellow is the color of all things joyful and vibrant. This happy color lifts our spirits. And if you want to improve your brain activity then make sure the blossoms are a clear, light yellow as this color improves our clarity of mind. In the Chinese geomantic tradition of feng shui, yellow is thought to enrich the emotions. In short, a yellow garden will help keep your spirits and energy high.

To create a cheery garden, plant lots of yellow flowers and foliage in the ground or in pots. There is a multitude of yellow plants to choose from. These include Goldfink coreopsis (*Coreopsis grandiflora* 'Goldfink'), dwarf 'Teddy Bear' sunflower (*Helianthus annuus* 'Teddy Bear'), dwarf black-eyed Susan (*Rudbeckia fulgida var. sullivantii* 'Goldsturm'), petunia 'Supertunia Citrus,' and golden creeping Jenny (*Lysimachia nummularia* 'Aurea'), among many others.

Top, left: *Pair gold mound spirea (Spiraea japonica 'Gold Mound') with yellow tulips for a happy pop in your garden in the spring. This effect is short-lived because the spirea will slowly turn yellow/green and the tulips will pass.*

Top, right: *The French marigold 'Safari Yellow' (Tagetes patula 'Safari Yellow') provides a constant and hassle-free annual flower display.*

Bottom: *Large blooms of the tropical 'Evangeline' hibiscus (Hibiscus rosa sinensis 'Evangeline') sport white and yellow single flowers with a ruby-red throat. This flower is suitable for a seasonal planter or warmer climates.* Photo by Laura McKillop.

77. WHY WHITE?

*White is not a mere absence of color; it is a shining and affirmative
thing, as fierce as red, as definite as black. God paints in many colors;
but He never paints so gorgeously, I had almost said so gaudily, as when
He paints in white."* —G. K. Chesterton

A predominantly white garden with snowy, opalescent flowers positively glows in the evening. White flowers and foliage calm us, and they create an uplifting atmosphere. White seems to embrace the form of a flower better than any other color. It shows off the shape pristinely.

We associate white gardens with simplicity and serenity. Pots of snowy white roses or mounded white lantana make gray mornings seem less gloomy. Similarly, snowball viburnums clad in white flowers light up dappled borders with their luminous spring show. The variety and type of white flowers you can grow is tremendous. It seems nature can never have too much white.

There are cool whites and warm whites in the plant world. Cool whites are clear and go with silvery foliage such as 'Miss Willmott's Ghost' sea holly (*Eryngium* 'Miss Willmott's Ghost'), 'Powis Castle' silver sage (*Artemisia arborescens* 'Powis Castle'), and gray-leaved lamb's ears (*Stachys byzantina*). Creamy whites are complemented by warmer greens such as lady's mantle and hydrangea.

White tulips planted in a large group at the aptly named White garden in Lewisboro, New York. It is open to the public two times a year through the Open Days program of the Garden Conservancy.

Clockwise: *White plants in masses make quite a statement. 'Deustchland' astilbe are striking when planted in a large group. It is a shade-loving perennial flower that blooms in spring.*

In fall, the perennial flower, Japanese anemone (Anemone x hybrid 'Honorine Jobert') sports brilliant white blooms with yellow centers.

The white pointed blossoms cover a Kousa dogwood tree (Cornus kousa) in late spring. They can be a real show stopper.

Yucca flowers (Yucca filimentosa) exhibit the sweetness of white against green leaves.

Top, left: *Paint your garden white with summer-blooming 'Iceberg' floribunda roses in pots. They are fragrant and bloom from early to mid-summer into fall.*

Top, right: *Siberian iris 'Butter & Sugar' (Iris sibirica 'Butter & Sugar') pops against a deep green backdrop of Blue Princess holly (Ilex x meserveae 'Blue Princess').*

Left: *'Sunny' Knockout roses blend beautifully with a white 'Limelight' Hydrangea (Hydrangea paniculata 'Limelight'). The added touch of yellow in the rose is a bonus.*

78. IN LOVE WITH ORANGE

Orange is a color that people either really enjoy or intensely dislike. There seems to be no in-between response to this vibrant color. It is a true stimulant—increasing oxygen to the brain, increasing our appetite, and exciting the emotions. In the words of Frank Sinatra, "Orange is the happiest color."

Orange, a bright and flamboyant color, comes into its own in the garden during the height of summer. Bold flowers such as orange daylilies, canna lilies, and marigolds radiate joy under the rays of the hot sun. Of course, this bright show is meant to entice pollinators. The brighter the flower, the more likely it will be visited. Butterflies especially like orange. As the days ripen into the coolness of fall, orange-tinted flowers and leaves exude a warm glow.

There are also the softer shades of orange such as peach, tangerine, and apricot that you can use in your plant beds. These mellow, warm tones blend beautifully with yellow and blue flowers. Gray-leaved plants such as dusty miller, dianthus, and santolina set off orange deliciously.

Orange-leaved plants include Scotch heather 'Copper Splendor' (*Calluna vulgaris* 'Copper Splendor'), Coppertina Ninebark (*Physocarpus opulifolius* 'Mindia'), and 'Orange Dream' Japanese maple (*Acer palmatum* 'Orange Dream').

I planted a row of orange-blooming canna lily against a muted gray wall of a modern home. Every summer their vibrant, tropical blooms light up the area and contrast beautifully with the exterior.

This happy meadow is made up of sun-loving peren-nials that bloom every year. Here orange poppies (Eschscholzia californica) blend beautifully with blue cornflower (Centaurea cyanus), Queen Anne's lace, and yellow tickseed (Coreopsis).

A group of orange Darwin hybrid tulips starts off the spring with a bang. With margins of yellow, it looks amazing when planted with yellow or purple tulips.

Left: *Deep orange daylilies (Hemerocallis) contrast boldly with blue campanulas. A perfect pairing for a sunny summer garden display.*

Facing page: *Orange comes into its own in the fall. Here orange chrysanthemums in planters add pizzazz to the landscape.*

79. A MATTER OF SUNLIGHT

Our color choices in the landscape are, for the most part, influenced by our geographic location and the time of year. In summer, the sun's intensity is strongest north of the equator, but in the northernmost areas of the earth the sun's rays are weaker than in more southerly areas. For example, in the muted, northern light of England pastel colors captivate while bright colors may appear garish. Thus, the famed British garden designer Gertrude Jekyll saw purple as a difficult color. Contrast this to a sunny subtropical garden, where the light is strong. There, every shade of purple and magenta is exuberantly appealing. It is all a matter of sunlight.

Similarly, our color preferences can change with the season. In early spring, when the light is soft, we thrill to light pink and soft yellow. As the year progresses, and the sun becomes stronger, pastels look washed out, and we crave stronger red, golds, and oranges outdoors. And, of course, the strength of the sun's rays changes with the time of day. In the morning and late afternoon, the sun's rays strike the earth at a low angle. At these times the light may be bright but not very intense. The sun is strongest from 11 a.m. to 3 p.m. There is indeed a time and a place for every color under the sun.

A mass of colorful pansies brightens up cloudy spring days. Photo by Laura McKillop.

The orange and pink found in the 'Magnus' coneflower (Echinacea purpurea 'Magnus') hold up well in the intense summer sun.

80. A POP OF RED

Bold. Bright. Pow.

Red, an eye-catching hue, stands up to the summer sun's withering glare. In a multicolored planting, warm colors always dominate, and while orange and yellow sing their hearts out, red always steals the show. In fact, if you want to make a distant flowerbed appear closer, include a large dose of red. As fabric designer and colorist Jack Lenor Larsen noted, "Of all the hues, reds have the most potency."

Did you know that bees can't see red? Red flowers are usually pollinated by birds, butterflies, hummingbirds, and the wind. So when you add some red into your garden, not only will you have the benefit of its pizazz, you might also attract red-loving hummingbirds.

There are many bright red flowers that will add pop to your garden. Red geraniums, red roses, and red tulips are traditional standards; but don't forget red cockscomb, red poppies, and red chrysanthemums. And, of course, red bridges, red gates, and red outdoor furniture will always be powerful attention getters in a landscape. If you want to spice up a garden, add a pop of red!

Clockwise: *A red, deer-resistant annual flower that grabs the eye is 'Strawberry Fields' gomphrena (Gomphrena haageana 'Strawberry Fields').*

The punchy red perennial coneflower 'Salsa Red' (Echinacea purpurea 'Salsa Red') is aptly named.

Add red to your garden in the fall by planting red pincushion chrysanthemums in a garden bed or pot. These have the added feature of a small yellow center.

Red New Guinea impatiens in planters add a bit of contrast to a shady scene.

81. ONE-COLOR GARDENS AND PLANTERS

You cannot go wrong when you combine flowers and foliage that are in the same color family. Monochromatic gardens and planters are alluring when they are swathed with one color or highlight subtle differences of a single hue. Blue gardens are especially popular, as are white gardens. We all seem to love one-color gardens, even if blue gardens include a bit of purple or white gardens have a touch of yellow. Of course, no matter what color you choose to spotlight, foliage will be a part of the mix. You can use foliage to your advantage in a monochromatic planting by including plants with green, gray, or variegated green and white leaves to act as a backdrop to the main color.

Containers featuring plants of one color are fun and easy to create. Planters filled with white flowers are especially eye-catching. For example, a combination of white lantana, white scaveola, and green and white 'Wojo's Jem' Vinca vine is cooling on a summer day. Blue planter schemes are also intriguing. You can combine blue wave petunias and a tall 'Heavenly Blue' morning glory, trained on a central lattice, for some blue perfection in a pot. And don't forget an all-pink planter packed with pink million bells, dark green ivy, and pink chrysanthemums.

Above: *A green garden features a dark green bench sitting within a bed of pachysandra (Pachysandra terminalis) and lacy lady ferns (Athyrium filix-femina). This is Phyllis Warden's garden in Bedford, New York. You can see this landscape through the Garden Conservancy Open Days program.*

Below: *A shiny, golden planter sits within bright yellow flowers at the Epcot International Flower & Garden Festival in Orlando, Florida.*

Above: *A planter can be a verdant accent in any setting. Here dark green caladium leaves contrast with the foliage of light green coleus and sweet potato vine* (Ipomoea batatas).

Left: *A green garden of goldmound spirea, juniper, and low-growing lady's mantle* (Alchemilla mollis) *along a stepping stone path is soothing.*

82. INVENTIVE AND CREATIVE—GREEN

Green, in all its shades and tones, is the tranquil color of nature. It is also the hue that has been found to stimulate creativity. Researchers at the University of Munich found that brief exposure to green appeared to activate inventiveness! Specifically, participants exposed to green outperformed those exposed to white, gray, red, and blue. They found that a glimpse of green instills "the type of pure, open (mental) processing required to do well on creativity tasks." Therefore, innovative thinking is stimulated by the color green. Wow.

The reason for this may be because green is the most restful color to our eyes. It balances us and alleviates anxiety. Perhaps we can relax better in a setting filled with green plants, and then our ideas can flow.

Knowing this, the next time you want to come up with a great idea, take a stroll through a park or spend some time in a garden where green plant textures and forms—rather than myriad colors—predominate. Envelop yourself in nature's green and think creative thoughts.

A shady area can become a sea of green. The large leaves of 'Guacamole' hosta have dark green margins while the centers become brighter gold in summer. It is accompanied by white-edged 'Francee' hosta, ostrich ferns (Mateuccia struthiopteris), golden Japanese forest grass (Hakonechloa macra 'Aureola') and a mass of the dark green native perennial, Mayapple (Podophyllum peltatum), in the rear.

83. SEE THE BASICS

To see things in black and white is to see the basics, and I would recommend to any designer of gardens that he go out and look at his work by the light of the moon. —Eleanor Perenyi

To see your garden by the moon is to reduce it to its bare essentials. Gardens seen on cloudy evenings or in moonlight are devoid of detail. The dim light seems to wash away the colors, leaving only the strong lines of the landscape discernible. It is a black, white, and gray world, like a grainy black-and-white photograph. This is what the American garden writer Eleanor Perenyi meant by "see the basics."

In low light, such as at dusk, strip an otherwise exuberant garden down to the bones. It is then that you can see the basics, because there is nothing to distract the eye. What a good time to assess how the overall layout holds together. Does your garden pass the "cloudy at dusk" test?

Montauk daisies (Nipponanthemum nipponicum) *shine in the light of an October moon, returning every year to put on a glorious fall show.*

White plants form the "basics" of a landscape in the evening. These plants brighten the shadows—'Ivory Halo' Tatarian dogwood (Cornus alba 'Bailhalo'), Japanese anemone 'Honorine Jobert' (Anemone x hybrida 'Honorine Jobert'), and large-leaf mountain mint (Pycnanthemum muticum).

Left: *A double-arched gate painted blue looks stately atop a Belgian block stone apron. The light color of the granite stone works well with the dark blue. The relatively long stone apron is in good proportion to the wide gate.*

Right: *This shady recessed gate is flanked by two tall boxwoods. The tall evergreen behind it is a yellow threadleaf cypress* (Chamacyparis pisifera '*Filifera Aurea*').

84. THE MYSTERY OF A BLUE GATE

Who says that fences and gates must be white? Or one solid color? Fences are useful, and their presence cannot always be hidden. So in the spirit of making the fence the show or simply enhancing what you already have, why not try a new color the next time you paint or stain a fence?

Deep blue gates add mystery to an outdoor space. They like to hide in the shadows, and you can enhance this shadowy desire by setting a gate back within foliage. This is because blue, especially dark blue, is a recessive color, which means it tends to fade into the background. When sunlight hits it, however, a deep blue gate will take its rightful place on stage. Once you see a blue gate you cannot help but go and check it out.

You can make the mysterious scene even more enticing if you plant yellow-leaved plants nearby. Golden hues contrast beautifully with blue and brighten up a space. Some good choices are yellow-leaved 'August Moon' hosta (*Hosta* 'August Moon'), 'Dart's Gold' Ninebark (*Physocarpus opulifolius* 'Dart's Gold'), and 'Sutherland Gold' Elderberry (*Sambucus racemosa* 'Sutherland Gold'), among many others.

85. PINK AND PURPLE—A DYNAMIC DUO

Purple speaks of magic and mystery. Pink represents nurturing and love. Who wouldn't want this sprightly combination in their garden? These sherbet colors add a romantic zing to any outdoor space.

One way to show off the pink and purple duo is to contrast bloom styles. For example, plant a large, open purple Jackman clematis vine against spikes of pink tulips. Once these spring bloomers pass, deep pink double Knock Out roses and upright, purple perennial salvia "Caradonna" can take their place. Another luscious combination in spring is a dark pink peony, purple iris, and a "Pink Supreme" Flower Carpet® rose.

Classic cottage gardens love pairing pink with purple. Purple adds richness to a scene while pink hints of innocence. Dark pink, light pink, lavender, and deep purple would be a "wow" color scheme. In fact, there are many shades of purple to play with. Violet purple is a vivid color. True purple looks great with pink. Dark purple tones down light pinks.

For a truly magnificent pink-and-purple display, plant a bountiful pairing of different shades of hydrangeas. They can bloom with round mopheads of pale pink to rich salmon and light purple—a rainbow of colors.

Top, left: *In spring, deep 'Purple Flag' tulips stand out against the clear pink blossoms of 'Olga Mezitt' PJM rhododendrons.*

Top, right: *The showy blooms of lantana 'Patriot Medium Pink,' a durable, deer-resistant annual in northern areas, combined with Scaveola 'Blue Wonder' and fine-leaved blue fescue (Festuca glauca) makes an eye-popping combo in a planter.*

Left: *In summer, the prolific purple globes of Gomphrena 'Buddy Purple' combine with the open flowers of annual vinca 'Titan Blush' (Catharanthus roseus 'Titan Blush'). Both are heat and drought tolerant, perfect for a sunny location.*

Left: *Multicolored zinnias "sing" in unison on a summer morning. Resilient annual plants, they like full sun and warm weather.*

Below: *The petunia variety, Surfinia 'Sky Blue,' mixes beautifully with the white foliage of lamium 'Beacon Silver,' tall white angelonia, dainty light 'Blue Star' (Laurentia axillaris 'Blue Star'), and small white calibrachoa. Fertilize several times throughout the summer to keep flowers singing.*

86. THE SOUND OF FLOWERS

The temple bell stops but I still hear the sound coming out of the flowers.
—Basho (Japanese poet, seventeenth century)

No matter how beautiful an outdoor space, it is always the pot or plant bed full of flowers that grabs the eye and garners the most praise. Using the metaphor of music, flowers add sweet tones to the symphony of a garden. It is their soaring melody, with notes of blue, pink, white, and more that we all enjoy.

Flowers bring delight that goes beyond pretty blossoms and sweet-smelling fragrance. Researcher Jeannette Haviland-Jones of Rutgers University found that flowers are a natural mood enhancer. Women who receive flowers reported more positive moods for three days, and a flower given to men or women in an elevator elicited more positive social behavior than other stimuli. Haviland-Jones wrote, "Science shows that not only do flowers make us happier than we know, they have strong positive effects on our emotional well-being."

I once read that, in the spring, Tibetans like to sit downwind from flowers so they can be dusted with the pollen from the new blossoms that floats on the spring breezes. It seems we all like flowers for the healing they bring us. It is the sound of flowers.

87. MATCH THAT LEAF!

There is a beautiful, red arched bridge at Michael Steinhardt's extensive landscape in Mount Kisco, New York. In the fall it perfectly matches the red foliage of a nearby threadleaf Japanese maple. The similarity of the colors is spectacular. If they were slightly different reds, the resulting contrast would be jarring because the colors would be "mismatched."

How do you ensure that a painted gate, door, or bridge matches the fall foliage in your garden? In this day of computerized matching of paint colors, the answer is surprisingly straightforward. Wait until a tree or shrub puts on its cloak of fall color and, at the peak, take a leaf to the paint store. The color analysis computer can make as close a match as possible. How great is that?

This is possible for flowers too. Imagine if you want to match a large mass of purple iris. Take a purple petal to the paint store and match it. Then bring the paint home to use on a piece of furniture, say a bench. You can place that purple bench near the purple iris bed. What a sight that might be!

You may be able to see the 58-acre Steinhardt Garden and its amazing collection of Japanese maples through the Garden Conservancy's Open Days Program. Go to their website for more information at www.gardenconservancy.org/open-days.

This deeply dissected red leaf of the Japanese maple (Acer palmatum 'Dissectum') matches the bridge color in the fall. The matching color effect is striking.

The matching colors of the arched bridge and foliage of the Japanese maple are beautifully accompanied by the slightly darker red of the reflection of the bridge in the water below.

Above: *The autumn foliage of dwarf foth-ergilla (Fothergilla major 'Mt. Airy') is outstanding. Leaves turn to fiery hues of orange and red with undertones of yellow.*

Right: *The colors of autumn include the deep burgundy of oakleaf hydrangeas (Hydrangea quercifolia) contrasted with the lime/yellow of 'Wasabi' coleus.*

88. BURNISHED COLORS OF LATE AUTUMN

The array of foliage colors in the fall brilliantly combines the glow of gold overlaid with deep crimson, soft green, hearty burgundy, and more. It is similar to the painting effect, called burnishing, which is the layering of multiple colors to create a rich, glazed appearance. Autumn foliage is burnished by nature. Leaves start to sport red, orange, or yellow tones that are then burnished with layers of deeper, warmer colors over time to become an almost iridescent copper or bronze. The metallic effect in late autumn is dazzling, especially when contrasted with verdant evergreens.

The fall is the best time to appreciate the varieties of color in a garden. The warm-hued plants coexist, side by side, to offer a scintillating mass of rich, earthy tones. The deep burgundy of oakleaf hydrangea and the yellow/orange foliage of witch hazel blend with the deep forest green of leatherleaf viburnums to exalt our senses on a sunny autumn day. Another burnished plant is dwarf fothergilla (*Fothergilla gardenia*). It provides a kaleidoscope of colors, sporting shades of purple, maroon, burgundy, red, orange, yellow, and gold. This color display is fleeting, a last gasp, before they drop. You must savor it when it appears.

89. ACCENT ON WHITE AND GREEN

White-leaved variegated plants don't seem to get the same attention as plants with white flowers. This is a shame, as sparkling white and green foliage lights up a garden bed like nothing else can. The white leaves of 'White Nancy' spotted dead nettle (*Lamium maculatum* 'White Nancy') or 'Jack Frost' Siberian bugloss (*Brunnera macrophylla* 'Jack Frost') are a lively addition to an all-green scene. Place them in front of a dark boxwood or yew backdrop, add a pop of red or an intriguing rock, and you have an elegant garden display.

The effectiveness of white-leaved plants depends on how many you plant and where they are located. A spot filled with a mass of the stunning groundcover, white-leaved 'Okina' lilyturf (*Liriope muscari* 'Okina'), cannot be beat. A grouping of the large white-and-green leaves of 'White Christmas' caladiums in the front of a shady bed is totally captivating. And the shade-loving 'Morning Sun' cast iron plant (*Aspidistra elatior* 'Asahi') stops visitors in their tracks with the dramatic white variegation in its tall leaves. It gets better as the season progresses, and the color holds all winter. For dry, deep shade and white foliage there isn't a better choice for a tough-as-nails perennial.

Luminescent creamy-white leaves of 'Moonlight' caladiums are edged in soft green. These low-maintenance plants look great when massed in shady gardens.

Clockwise: *Begonia rex 'Escargot' has spiral markings that are unique. The leaves circle inward to make each one look like a snail. (2) The narrow leaves with broad, cream stripes adorn 'Evergold' golden sedge (Carex hachijoensis 'Evergold'). Deer and disease resistant, this white-and-green sedge is long-lasting and easy to grow. (3) Nasturtium 'Alaska Mixed' (Tropaeolum majus 'Alaska mixed') has edible flowers and attractive white-and-green leaves. (4) 'Silver Heart' Siberian bugloss (Brunnera macrophylla 'Silver Heart') has heart-shaped leaves that are mostly white with a light green border. This tough perennial has cobalt blue, forget-me-not flowers. Perfect for woodland settings as a groundcover.*

The blue color of the pendulous branches of the weeping blue Atlas cedar (Cedrus atlantica
'Glauca Pendula') is breathtaking. Plant it next to other blue plants such as 'Elijah Blue'
fescue (Festuca glauca 'Elijah Blue'). The marked contrast of the delicate blue grass with
dense evergreen boughs is captivating.

90. THE SIREN CALL OF BLUE EVERGREENS

Blue needle-leafed conifers are in a class by themselves. Their vivid blue foliage thrills the eye, and they serve as a year-round centerpiece among seasonally changing plantings. You can mix blue-toned evergreens in your foundation planting where they will add winter interest. Use a compact variety that won't outgrow its space, like the wonderful 'Blue Shag' Eastern white pine (*Pinus strobus* 'Blue Shag'). Its dense, dwarf habit with soft, blue/green needles goes well with flowers and other plants.

One of the best blue evergreens is the weeping blue Atlas cedar (*Cedrus atlantica* 'Glauca Pendula'), which has branches that cascade like a slow moving, azure waterfall. Weeping Atlas cedar will grow to a height of 6 to 15 feet and a width of at least 15 feet, so consider carefully where you plant it. It can be trained and pruned to fit a smaller garden, but keep it away from walks or driveways where its outstretched branches might intrude.

Other outstanding blue evergreens to consider are the silvery-blue Boulevard cypress (*Chamaecyparis pisifera* 'Boulevard'), Blue Star juniper (*Juniperus squamata* 'Blue Star'), and Blue Creeper Juniper (*Juniperus scopulorum* 'Monam'), whose distinguished blue foliage intensifies its coloring in winter.

*Montgomery blue spruce (*Picea pungens 'Montgomery'*) is an excellent shrub for rock gardens. Here I softened it with the bright green, scalloped-edged leaves of 'Hummelo' betony (*Stachys officinalis 'Hummelo'*).*

91. VIBRANT DISPLAY IDEAS FOR FALL

In the fall, chrysanthemums are used to create a late-season display in pots and gardens. But you can expand autumn's palette with ornamental kale and cabbages, late-blooming asters, Montauk daisies, *Amaranthus,* and grasses.

Ornamental cabbages and kales come in shades of purple, pink, green, and white, and they look more like large flowers than vegetables. They tolerate cold weather and are easy to grow, making them perfect for fall containers and gardens. They can be eaten but are not as tasty as edible varieties. Ornamental cabbage stays low to the ground and has smooth scalloped leaves whereas ornamental kale varieties are taller, have serrated or fringed leaf margins, and hold their color better.

Amaranthus is a songbird's delight, as its fluffy plumes are full of nutritious seeds. Make sure to grow this for the birds and you. Ornamental grasses come in all colors and sizes, add height to the fall garden, and pair well with almost anything. 'Fireworks' fountain grass (*Pennisetum setaceum* 'Fireworks') has leaves with a deep maroon/purple center vein flanked by hot pink margins. Its bright color is perfect for a vivid fall display.

Top: *The long, pointed plumes of an Amaranthus last for many weeks on the plant, delighting songbirds that feast on their seeds all fall. It looks good silhouetted against a wall or a wood post. Wherever you plant it, the birds will find it.*

Bottom, left: *Scarlet kale (*Brassica oleracea acephala *'Scarlet') is both edible and decorative. After the plants are touched by a frost, its leaves turn a stunning shade of deep violet purple and wrinkle and curl, creating the textured look they are known for. Combine with cabbage, asters, mums, and grasses, as shown here.*

Bottom, right: *'Opopeo' Amaranthus has beautiful, large, deep red, upright flower spikes that are a knockout in fall. This Mexican heirloom also has tasty leaves that are tender when picked young.*

Left: *Multicolored planters capture the eye, especially when placed in front of a gray stone backdrop.*

Right: *White Shasta daisies* (Chrysanthemum x superbum) *grow next to pink, orange, and yellow 'Profusion' zinnias, blue annual salvia, and pink phlox. Color sings in diversity in the garden.*

92. PLAYING WITH COLORS

Gardening is how I relax. It's another form of creating
and playing with colors. —Oscar de la Renta

If you cannot play with color in a garden, where can you play? Sometimes we shy away from bright colors or clashing mixes in our everyday life but, outside in a garden, you can be as free and daring as you want.

Who says you can't mix red with magenta or blue with orange? Go ahead, plant that purple 'Profusion' zinnia next to the bright red cockscomb and see what happens. Or contrast maroon/red foliage of 'Summer Wine' Ninebark (*Physocarpus opulifolius* 'Summer Wine') with the clear pink of deciduous azaleas. If you don't like it, you can dig it up and move it. If nothing else, you will spark some lighthearted garden party discussions.

Bright colors are great for drawing attention to areas you want to highlight, like a front entrance. A scintillating color combination that people like is lime green and purple. It sounds terrible but when used in close proximity, they intensify one another. Try Purple Pixie® Fringe Flower (Loropetalum chinense 'Peack') underlined with the bright chartreuse cascading leaves of 'Margarita' sweet potato vine (*Ipomoea batatas* 'Margarita') or the grassy EverColor 'Everillo' Carex (*Carex oshimensis* 'EverColor® Everillo'). Go Bold.

Color cacophony! Shiny planters of various colors can coexist. To cool it off, add the trailing
'Silver Falls' dichondra (Dichondra argentea 'Silver Falls') as they did here at Epcot in
Orlando, Florida.

93. PAINT IT BLACK

I must admit I love garden sheds that are painted black. This severe yet intriguing color transforms a utilitarian structure into an elegant point of interest. Black can hide imperfections, because darker shades reflect less light than lighter colors. The dark color also minimizes a structure's impact on the landscape. It is like wearing black clothing—it puts attention elsewhere.

A black garden shed offers unique opportunities to have fun with trim colors. The border around a roof, window, or door can be painted in a contrasting color for additional "pop." Add a colorful planter in front of the black backdrop and you have a winning combination. Other good ideas are to hang a colorful hose on the wall, place blue or white chairs in front, or use a black paint with high sheen for a glossy effect.

The best part of a black garden shed is that you can use it as a backdrop for plants and pots. Train climbing white roses, like 'Iceberg' climbing rose, on it and place a white planter by the door. You can have a lot of fun with this. Paint it black.

This shiny black garden shed has the added interest of a red roof. This is at the Tuin de Villa in the Netherlands. Designed by the owners Lily and Fried Frederix. Photo by Laura McKillop.

Before and After—the verdict is in: paint it black.

5.

PLANTS
and
PLANTING

My heart found its home long ago in the beauty,
mystery, order and disorder of the flowering earth.

—Lady Bird Johnson
(founder, Lady Bird Johnson Wildflower Center)

The best part of a garden is undoubtedly its plants. They add the dynamic life energy that makes a garden "sing." Plants in all their myriad forms, colors, and flowers, provide the "beauty, mystery, order and disorder" that Lady Bird Johnson referred to. Whether they are in pots or in the ground, the presence of plants makes a space come alive.

But what plants should you include in your garden? This is a lifelong fascination for gardeners. There is always something else we want to add. But just as there are plant enthusiasts who lust after the latest cultivar, there are others who simply want their outdoor space to look good. Similarly, there are two kinds of plant buyers. The first group goes to a nursery with a plan and a corresponding plant list that spells out the quantity, size, and variety to be bought. The second group walks through the rows looking at this and that, hoping for some inspiration to help them choose the right plant for the space. Whichever group you belong to, a little plant knowledge goes a long way.

To help you in your selections, I am sharing a few of my favorite go-to plants. It is an eclectic group, with plants that can fit a wide range of gardens. Of course, there are many more plants that I can suggest, but space limits me. Hopefully, this section inspires you to consider these plants and encourages you to find others that suit your particular site. Make sure you know what USDA Plant Hardiness Zone you live in. A map is available online at planthardiness.ars.usda.gov/PHZMWeb.

Most of the plants featured in this section are relatively hardy and easy to grow. I am familiar with these plants because I live in the Northeast United States (USDA Zone 6) and have the most experience with them. I encourage you to explore the planting options available in your area and climate.

I have also added tips for planting and maintenance. These suggestions are important gardening pointers, such as how to improve the quality of your soil. I cannot write effusively about plants without talking about the soil.

Although the plants and planting section is last in *Gardentopia*, it may be the section that garden lovers go to first. I hope you use these suggested plants as a starting point and then add your own favorites to an ever-growing list. Happy gardening!

Opposite: Lamb's ear has lavender flowering stems that are a boon for the bees. Use them as cut flowers and pair with roses, peonies, or dahlias for a striking arrangement.

94. WHY WE GARDEN

The lesson I have thoroughly learnt, and wish to pass on to others,
is to know the enduring happiness that the love of a garden gives.
—Gertrude Jekyll

Why do we love to garden? Ball Horticultural Company conducted a survey and found that we garden for beauty first and relaxation second. In essence, we enjoy creating a beautiful outdoor space and savor the calm it bestows upon us. Gertrude Jekyll, the famed English garden writer and designer, put it more succinctly when she said that the love of a garden brings us happiness.

I have always thought that we garden for the good feelings it generates. We delight in connecting with the marvelous green world. It exalts the spirit. We look at a special tree, a zucchini plant, an evergreen shrub, or a simple flower and, for a moment, our worldly cares disappear. We are in the realm of the plants.

We garden to daydream, to enjoy the earth, and to be healed. It is here where we have an opportunity to co-create with nature. Our hands get dirty and our minds are at ease. And to top it off, we end up creating beauty and food. This, in a nutshell, is why we garden.

Top: *The tools of a gardener. We garden to connect with the earth and to enjoy its bounty. It calms us and heals us on a deep level.*

Bottom: *Bright, multicolored zinnias bloom happily at the height of summer along with the feathery blue Russian sage (*Perovskia atriplicifolia*) and compact perennial black-eyed Susan (*Rudbeckia fulgida sullivantii *'Goldsturm').*

95. BOTTLEBRUSH BUCKEYE

One of my favorite shrubs for woodland gardens is the handsome bottle-brush buckeye (*Aesculus parviflora*). This large plant, native to the south-eastern United States, has broad compound leaves and exotic long, white flower clusters held above the foliage like fluffy candles in early July. It grows to 8 feet tall and tends to sucker, so it may grow to be quite wide. Allow a lot of room for this remarkable understory plant. It is suited for USDA Zones 5–9 and has no serious foliage or pest problems.

Bottlebrush buckeye is perfect for partial shade conditions but can tolerate full sun for a part of the day in the northern USDA zones. Its out-standing feature is the profusion of erect, 12-inch-long, pointed, white flowers that resemble a bottlebrush. When it blooms in early summer there is nothing to match it. Place it at the woodland edge and you will enjoy the summer show every year.

The fall color of the bottlebrush buckeye is also a show stopper. The large, green leaves that cover the broad shrub turn a glorious buttery yellow. It is easy to grow and requires moist, well-drained soil.

Top: *Bottlebrush buckeye* (Aesculus parviflora) *can grow to be a wide-spreading planting as seen here. It is effective as a deciduous screen planting.*

Bottom: *Bottlebrush buckeye is planted behind a rustic railing. The flowers rise above the foliage. This is at Olana, the historic home and gardens of Hudson Valley painter Frederic Church, in Hudson, New York.*

Top, left: *This stunning symphony of groundcovers and ferns is in Phyllis Warden's garden in Bedford, New York. Red-leaved Perilla (Perilla frutescens) contrast with white and green 'Jack Frost' Brunnera (Brunnera macrophylla 'Jack Frost'), Japanese painted fern (Athyrium niponicum pictum), and the lime-colored bleeding heart (Dicentra spectabilis 'Gold Heart').*

Top, right: *Variegated Japanese sweet flag (Acorus gramineus 'Ogon'), a sedge-like perennial, meshes beautifully with dark green dwarf mondo grass (Ophiopogon japonicus 'Nana'). This variety of sweet flag has gold and green variegation and grows from 10 to 12 inches tall. Sweet flag has sweet-scented leaves, hence its name.*

Left: *'Plum Cascade' Heucherella and 'Green Spice' Coral Bells (Heuchera americana 'Green Spice') blend beautifully with the spiky blades of variegated Yucca 'Color Guard' (Yucca filamentosa 'Color Guard') and the gray-toned foliage of yellow 'Moonshine' yarrow.*

96. A FOLIAGE TAPESTRY

Isn't it interesting that nature, if given a choice, will cover the ground with a mix of many species growing side by side? This is the opposite of what we normally do, which is to plant a large mass of one low-growing plant as a groundcover. But nature works differently. Look at a forest floor and you can find a community of mosses, lichens, sedges, and other plants so tightly intertwined that they allow little room for any weed.

Many plant professionals today suggest we follow nature's lead and plant a conglomeration of different foliage and groundcover plants that have the same growth rate (no plant thugs!) and like the same site conditions. The key is diversity. If you don't mind some tending, a combination of small-leaved groundcovers with large-leaved foliage plants can be downright captivating.

Plant a few varieties of groundcovers together to create the effect of an interwoven tapestry. Allow them to grow into the other. For example, in a half shade woodland try sweet woodruff (*Galium odoratum*), violets, dwarf hostas, saxifrage, and woodland phlox (*Phlox divaricata*). It is a grand experiment to find those that like each other.

*Silvery lamb's ears (*Stachys byzantina *'Helen von Stein') mixed with coleus and dark green boxwood.*

97. RUSSIAN SAGE—PLAYS WELL WITH OTHERS

Russian sage (*Perovskia atriplicifolia*) is a hardy, deer-resistant perennial with lavender/blue flowers that thrives on neglect (USDA Zone 4–9). Perhaps its resilience is why it was named the Perennial Plant of the Year by the Perennial Plant Association way back in 1995. Its long-lasting spires of feathery flowers and silvery, aromatic foliage on upright stems are a fantastic addition to any summer and fall garden. It blooms from July through September.

This no-fuss plant grows from 2 to 4 feet tall and loves dry, sunny conditions and well-drained soil. It makes an excellent companion to ornamental grasses. The airy haze of soft blue works well against summer flowers like coneflowers, black-eyed Susans, perennial blue salvia, and Carefree Delight® roses.

For an unusual pairing, try Russian sage with bold foliage plants like yuccas and agaves. They all like the heat, and the contrast between the delicate, filigree blooms and sculptural agaves is eye-catching. Perfect for a silver/blue garden!

There are many varieties of *Perovskia*. 'Blue Spires' Russian sage is a vigorous 48-inch-tall variety with long blooming, dark blue flower spikes. The compact, 30 to 34-inch-high "Blue Jean Baby" is one of the earliest Russian sages to bloom. Its spires of purple flowers appear in midsummer and last until fall. Plant in a mass for a stunning effect.

Black-eyed Susans and Russian sage add a naturalized look to a meadow, hillside, or other sunny spot. Both tough plants, their abundant blooms in midsummer extend into fall.

98. COOL-SEASON VERSUS WARM-SEASON GRASSES

Why do some ornamental grasses look their best in the summer while others brown out? The answer is temperature. Some grasses love the heat while others prefer cooler times of year. Grasses are therefore classified as warm-season or cool-season.

Cool-season grasses are happiest in spring when the days are cool. These have their brightest foliage early in the year and combine beautifully with spring bulbs. By early summer, in hot, dry weather, their growth slows and they may go dormant. Popular cool-season grasses include blue fescue (*Festuca glauca*), blue oat grass (*Helictotrichon sempervirens*), and tufted hair grass (*Deschampsia cespitosa*).

Warm-season grasses thrive at temperatures in the 80 to 95°F range. They begin their growth later in the year and remain attractive until frost. They include northern sea oats (*Chasmanthium latifolium*), Japanese silver grass (*Miscanthus sinensis*), perennial fountain grass (*Pennisetum alopecuroides*), and switchgrass (*Panicum virgatum*). These grasses require less water and should be cut back to about 4 to 8 inches above ground in the early spring.

A versatile warm-season grass is the 'Karl Foerster' Feather Reed Grass (*Calamagrostis acutiflora* 'Karl Foerster'). It is a strongly upright grass that grows up to 5 feet tall. It was named the Perennial Plant of the Year in 2001 by the Perennial Plant Association.

Top: *Dwarf fountain grass* (Pennisetum alopecuroides 'Hameln'), *a warm-season grass, shows off its decorative flowerheads while maiden grass* (Miscanthus sinensis 'Gracillimus') *towers over it to the right.*

Bottom: *The feathery flowers of the tall zebra grass* (Miscanthus sinensis 'Zebrinus') *blow in the breeze on a clear September day. Warm-season grasses such as this are at their peak from late summer into fall, requiring little care. Deer resistant too.* Photo by Laura McKillop.

99. BUTTERFLY WEED—SO IMPORTANT

The 2017 Perennial Plant of the Year was butterfly weed (*Asclepias tuberosa*). The Perennial Plant Association chose this long-lived, native prairie flower because it is both beautiful and a butterfly magnet. Butterfly weed is a hardy perennial with a large taproot.

Its vibrant orange flowers reach two feet high and make an eye-popping display when planted in large masses. It thrives in a sunny garden with average to dry soil. It is suited to USDA Zones 3–9.

Butterfly weed certainly lives up to its name, attracting a wide range of butterflies, bumblebees, honeybees, and hummingbirds to the abundant nectar that it produces. A member of the milkweed family, it is occasionally used by monarch butterflies as a caterpillar food plant.

Our insects are in peril, and that is why we should help butterfly weed to grow and spread. It is easily propagated by seed. The fruit is a pod that will split open when it ripens in the fall—the seeds are attached to a tuft of silky white hairs. You can open the fully ripened pods and let the seeds float away on the breeze. These seeds need a three-month cold stratification. Therefore, plant the seed in autumn in order to germinate the following spring.

The big orange flower heads of butterfly weed burst into bloom in mid to late summer. It is especially attractive to monarch butterflies, acting as a nectar source. The decorative blooms are a long-lasting cut flower.

It takes 2 to 3 years before butterfly weed (Asclepias tuberosa) produces its flowers. Once established, it lasts for years, becoming thicker each year.

100. ROSETTE PATTERNS GRAB THE EYE

Plants with radial foliage always grab our attention in the garden. "Rosette" is the term used to describe a circular pattern of leaves that emerge out from the center with a wheel-like symmetry. A rosette plant usually has leaves that start near the ground. Several types of plants grow in this intriguing way.

Some succulent plants, those that store water in their thickened leaves, grow in a rosette pattern. This radial formation of leaves allows maximum exposure to the sun and captures any moisture and directs it down toward the roots. How effective! In temperate areas, you can enjoy the rosette patterns of the plant known as hens and chicks (*Sempervivum* spp.). In warmer areas, USDA zones 8 and above, you can grow rosette pattern plants such as aloe (*Aloe* spp.) and agave (*Agave* spp.).

A few garden vegetables, such as lettuce, cabbage, and kale form rosettes but lose that shape when they form flowers as the temperature or light increases.

Top, left: *Mexican snowball (Echeveria elegans) is a warm-zone succulent that forms a tight rosette of gray leaves. These plants spread through offshoots that can grow in and around rocks, as shown.*

Top, right: *Aeonium are succulent plants with spoon-shaped foliage. This genus comes in shades of burgundy, green, or variegated foliage. Some species like Aeonium arboretum are treelike and have woody stems that branch out to a height of 2 to 3 feet. Each is topped with rosettes of shiny green foliage.*

Bottom: *The desirable Blue Rose Echeveria (Echeveria imbricata) has tight rosettes of light blue/green leaves tinged with pink on the outer edges. This attractive Mexican native bears clusters of red flowers from spring to early summer. Great in both planters and in rock gardens, it is a frost-tender evergreen.*

101. THE LOVELY SMOKEBUSH

Smokebush (*Cotinus coggygria*) is named for the hazy purplish-pink puffs of "smoke" that cover this upright, multistemmed shrub throughout the summer. The smoke is really the delicate and profuse hairs that are attached to spent flower clusters. It is not the flowers that catch our attention but the spent billowy blooms.

The "smoke" is not the only thing that makes this deciduous shrub such a standout. It is the dark reddish-colored leaves that are so marvelous in a garden. As Henry Mitchell, a garden writer known as the Earthman, opined in his book *The Essential Earthman: Henry Mitchell on Gardening*, ". . . and then I have my favorite plants whose mission is not so much to bloom as to have good-looking leaves." Yay for shrubs with good-looking leaves!

The cultivars of smokebush known for colored foliage include the burgundy-leaved 'Royal Purple' and the purple-leaved 'Velvet Cloak.' These do not flower as reliably as the green-leaved smokebush varieties. For the best color foliage, cut the shrub back in early spring to within 2 to 3 feet of the ground. This may seem drastic but the deer-resistant plant grows back fast and will be covered in deep wine-red or purple leaves, depending on the cultivar. Please note that if you prune it hard you will lose the flowers and the "smoke" of its spent flowers. But as Mitchell said, the aim is to have "good-looking leaves."

*The fall foliage of smokebush (*Cotinus coggygria*) sport attractive shades of yellow, orange, and purplish-red. The colors are best in a sunny location.*

Gardentopia

Above: *Smokebush is native from southern Europe to central China. It is deer resistant and can be planted as a single specimen or as an informal mass. When planted to hide something, you can call it a smoke screen.*

Below: *The large, oval burgundy leaves of 'Royal Purple' smokebush make a dark-leaved contrast, especially planted in front of dense evergreens such as an emerald green arborvitae.*

102. THE LIFE OF THE WORLD

*Nothing that lives is, or can be, perfect; part of it is decaying, part
nascent. The foxglove blossom—a third part bud, a third part past,
a third part in full bloom, is a type of the life of the world.*
—John Ruskin

We should not only celebrate the flower and bud but also the beauty in the older and decaying blossom. This was a part of the philosophy of John Ruskin, an English reformer and philosopher born in the early nineteenth century. He was a champion of seeing beauty in all things, and he placed nature as the true standard. Examples of beauty and grace include clouds at sunset, trees bending in the wind, and the foxglove.

In this poignant quote, he counsels us to see beauty in all aspects of nature's life cycle and to honor it. Nature is ever-changing. Nothing is perfect nor static. As Ruskin sagely notes, we should celebrate the "third part past" that is, after all, a part of the life of the world in which we live. The past is the fading leaves, the spent blossom, and the lichen-covered stone. It is the quiet aftermath of spring's effervescence and summer's bounty.

Moss grows around natural wood rounds. They will eventually decompose as time goes on. Notice the exuberant ostrich ferns in the background.

103. STEPPED HEDGES FOR A SLOPING SITE

Formal hedges that are neatly trimmed add a precise, clean look to a landscape. Hedge plants such as boxwood, privet, and yew can be carefully pruned with straight edges and perfect corners. Rather than trusting your eye, you can set up a string guideline to help you maintain the rigid lines when pruning the top and the sides. Insert a strong stake into the ground at each end of the hedge that you are trimming. Tie the string onto each stake at the height you want to trim the hedge. This process requires focus but it is so satisfying when seeing a hedge all trimmed.

Slopes present a challenge for hedges, so why not prune a hedge in stepped tiers? This horticultural technique transforms a line of plants into an architectural feature in the garden. The stepped foliage creates a shadow at each drop that is an attractive feature. Determine the location and height of each tier, set the string line, and prune carefully for stepped hedges. Start at one end (never start in the middle), use a light touch, and do not trim off too much foliage in one pass. Beware of dips in the ground, which can cause dips in your cut.

Stepped hedges can be accentuated by different levels but it is the shadows that make them stand out.

104. LAMB'S EAR—BEAUTIFUL AND USEFUL

Lamb's ear (*Stachys byzantina*), an old-fashioned garden plant, is known for its soft, fuzzy silver-gray leaves that resemble the shape of a lamb's ear. The felty leaves are so inviting that you cannot pass it by without being tempted to give the leaves a quick touch. Lamb's ears is no higher than 15 inches tall, and it is easily grown in well-drained soils in full sun or part shade. It is a garden favorite because it is rabbit and deer resistant and can grow on dry and shallow to rocky soil. It is a rapidly growing and memorable plant that anyone in USDA Zones 4–8 can grow!

In the garden, lamb's ears is a fluffy, silvery accent that can be used in the front of a bed. The lavender flowers are not showy, but the bees like it. It is also a perfect groundcover under roses, mixed with catmint (*Nepeta*) and perennial geraniums. Look for varieties like 'Big Ears,' 'Silver Carpet,' and the wonderful 'Helen Von Stein.' The last one has better summer foliage than the rest and rarely produces flowering stems.

Lamb's ears has been used for centuries as a wound dressing. The leaves are antibacterial, anti-inflammatory, and help blood to clot more quickly. How useful, nature's bandage!

'Helen Von Stein' lamb's ear grows quickly, rarely flowers, and takes heat well. It is perfect as a deer-resistant plant and adds a soft touch hanging over a stone wall. A true workhorse in the garden.

105. THE GIFT OF THE GARDENIA

Did you know that we share the same fragrance preferences as honeybees? We are both lured to the flowery scents of rose, jasmine, and gardenia, which are also the most popular fragrances in perfumery. Maybe we prefer these scents because they have an immediate impact on our sense of well-being. When we sniff a gardenia, the scent crosses directly from our nose into our brain and uplifts our mood quickly. In fact, the scent of the velvety white blossoms of gardenia (*Gardenia jasminoides*) is said to have an antidepressant effect.

I always have a gardenia shrub in a large planter by my back door in summer. I sniff it every day when I go to work in the morning and when I come home in the evening. I call the complex fragrance of the flowers "nature's mood enhancer." That is the gift of the gardenia.

A wonderful variety is 'August Beauty.' It is a 5-foot-high, rounded shrub with profuse, fragrant blooms. Patio tree forms are perfect for planters and are suitable for USDA Zones 8–11. A gardenia that can survive in cold areas is 'Summer Snow.' This hybrid grows 4 to 5 feet tall and wide in full to partial sun and grows in USDA Zones 6–11.

The captivating fragrance of the gardenia bush can be appreciated along pathways, near windows, and by entryways. Plant several in a line along a walkway.

Left: *A good example of cloud pruning of pine trees can be seen at the Japanese garden in the Huntington Gardens in San Marino, California.*

Below: *Pines, with their wide diversity of shape and size, can be pruned into open "cloud" forms where the inner structure is revealed and the wide spreading branches accentuated.*

106. CLOUD PRUNING

I love the term *cloud pruning*. It refers to a distinctive form of tree and shrub pruning from Japan that accentuates a plant's branch structure to create "clouds" of foliage. This plant-trimming tradition, called *Niwaki*, has been used over the centuries to make plants appear more like sculptural accents.

Cloud pruning is like a layered haircut. The branches are clipped to reveal glimpses of interior stems while foliage is trimmed into organic, rounded shapes, often in tiers. Similar to topiary pruning that makes plants sport "pom poms" like a poodle, *Niwaki* is more subtle. The aim is to allow sunlight to penetrate inside the plant and make the foliage appear as floating clouds.

Plants with a horizontal growing habit such as boxwood, azaleas, Chamaecyparis, laceleaf Japanese maples, and pines are among the most suitable for cloud pruning. You can also try cloud pruning on Osmanthus (*Osmanthus x burkwoodii*) and glossy-leaved holly. Go slow and remember that it is easy to cut but impossible to replace!

This golden full moon Japanese maple (Acer shirasawanum 'Aureum') has been lightly pruned to enhance its delicate form.

107. SNOWFLAKE OAKLEAF HYDRANGEA

Oakleaf hydrangea (*Hydrangea quercifolia*) is a native, part-shade plant known for its large, deeply lobed leaves and long, white panicle flowers. 'Snowflake' is a gorgeous cultivar of oakleaf hydrangea (*Hydrangea quercifolia* 'Brido'), and its stunning intricate blossoms produce tiers of new sepals over older ones, resembling double flowers. As these showy, sterile flowers age, they create a two-toned color effect of white and dusty purple/pink, which make them a real eye catcher! The large blooms emerge in July and last for 6 to 8 weeks. Snowflake hydrangea grows 5 to 8 feet tall and wide.

'Snowflake' is considered by many to be the most beautiful of the oakleaf hydrangeas. Introduced into cultivation in the early 1970s by Aldridge Nursery in Alabama, it grows in USDA Zones 5–9. In the fall, the leathery foliage turns a deep burgundy with hints of purple and crimson. It holds on to its leaves into December, and when the leaves drop, cinnamon-colored peeling bark is revealed. Plant this in a prominent, full-sun to part-shade location to enjoy the summer show. Highly recommended!

'Snowflake' oakleaf hydrangea flowers have remarkable intricate flowers that can be admired up close. It blooms on old wood, so do not cut back in the spring. It needs little pruning.

Top: *The enormous 15-inch-long white panicles of 'Snowflake' oakleaf hydrangea (Hydrangea quercifolia 'Brido') can extend upward, outward, or hang down. Here they point up in July and then, later in the summer, droop down gracefully.*

Bottom: *The cultivar 'Snowflake' was discovered in 1969 by Eddie Aldridge and his father in the Alabama woodlands. The duo, noted for their work with hydrangeas, propagated it and it is now the signature flower of Aldridge Gardens in Hoover, Alabama. It is a great public garden to visit.*

Left: *Variegated Solomon's Seal (Polygonatum odoratum pluriflorum 'Variegatum') likes moist conditions and shade. Slowly spreads to form colonies in optimum growing conditions. This was the Perennial Plant Association's 2013 Perennial Plant of the Year. Makes quite the impression!*

Below: *'White Lava' elephant ears (Colocasia esculenta 'White Lava') steal the show at Dallas Arboretum and Botanical Garden. It is a tightly clumping variety that is ideal for mass planting a garden bed.*

108. A LOT OF A LITTLE

Did you ever notice how a garden can become a jumble of plants? There is one of this and one of that, all growing into the other. The look is a little disconcerting. You can create order out of this chaos by planting fewer varieties in large masses. In other words, plant lots of a few things. Limit yourself to your favorite flowers, foliage, or shrubs. Plant them in large drifts of nine or more of one plant. It may sound like that is too much but the large swath will dominate the scene and make a memorable impression. You can try this with astilbes, hostas, or iris. As you'll see, "massing" can be quite effective.

I once heard that the famed Dutch plantsman and designer, Piet Oudolf, designer of New York's High Line gardens, would sometimes add a zero to the quantity originally noted on his plant list. So if there were eight plants specified, he would later change it to 80. I am not sure that is true but it is a way to make a visual statement!

So resist the urge to plant too many different plants. Just remember this adage: Plant a lot of a little.

109. EMBRACE THE MOSS

If you have a shady yard, do not despair. Make moss your friend and encourage its spread. Moss creates a velvety evergreen mat and can thrive at the base of tree trunks, on stone, and on compacted soil. It will grow year-round if you give it moisture. Without water, it will go dormant. Mosses grow on soils with a wide range of pH, but acid soils are best.

You can introduce moss in a garden or transplant it any time of the year as long as consistent moisture is available. I collect moss from one part of a yard and move it to another shady spot, then I lightly water with a fine mist spray. Watering the moss often is essential after you plant it. The best time of day to water is in the morning. Once it becomes happy in its new location, the moss will continue to spread naturally.

Moss evokes special responses in people. When Rikyu, a sixteenth-century Japanese tea ceremony master, was asked what constituted the perfect tea garden, he replied, "Thick green moss, all pure and sunny warm." There is nothing as luxuriant in a garden as a thick blanket of moss.

Left: *Moss grows around the native wildflower spotted wakerobin (Trillium maculatum), creating a living mulch. To do this, plant the wildflowers first before you introduce mosses. They both grow naturally on forests floors and onstream banks.*

Right: *Moss slowly grows up the stone steps we built in a woodland garden. Moss can be slippery underfoot so be careful about letting it spread on walkways and steps.*

Above: *The drought-tolerant 'Vera Jameson' sedum makes a great edging in front of other sun lovers, like this 'Magic Carpet' rose.* Photo by Laura McKillop.

Below: *'Sparkler' sedge (Carex phyllocephala 'Sparkler') is a delightful and low-maintenance perennial that grows in USDA Zones 7–10. Its green-and-white leaves look like fireworks as it brightens a shady garden bed.* Photo by Laura McKillop.

110. PLANTS IN THE FRONT ROW

The plants at the visible edge along a walk, patio, or lawn can make all the difference in its appearance. I suggest you plant low-growing plants in what I call the front row so as to accentuate the shape of the bed, soften harsh edges, and help to feature the taller plants that may be located behind them.

The preferred height of plants for the front row of a garden bed depends on the bed's location. For example, if you view a garden bed from afar, the height of the edging plants can be relatively high, such as 18 to 24 inches. This is because low-growing plants may not be visible from a distance. However, in plant beds that are viewed up close, the front of the border plants should be lower, about 6 to 12 inches high.

Low-growing plants in the front row of a bed that edge a walkway should be full, look good in a line, and not require too much care. Annuals such as sweet alyssum make a wonderful edging with its dense, tiny, fragrant white flowers. If cut back, they will bloom all season. The perennial green-and-white variegated lilyturf (*Liriope muscari* 'Variegata') is another favorite for edging beds. Other options include myrtle (*Vinca minor*), lady's mantle (*Alchemilla mollis*), and small astilbes.

Low-growing boxwood shaped as small globes make a neat and intriguing edge along a stone walk.

111. THE PURPLE PERSIAN SHIELD

We all love purple leaves! One of the best purple-leaf plants is Persian shield (*Strobilanthes dyerianus*). A striking foliage plant from tropical Myanmar, it has spectacular, long pointed purple, iridescent purple, and dark green leaves. It is a tender small shrub, hardy in USDA Zones 9–11, that can grow 3 feet high. In cool climates it makes a great annual in planters and beds. It thrives on heat and humidity and sports the most color in partially shaded locations. Best of all, deer or rabbits do not like Persian shield!

These easy-care plants look great right up until the first frost. Use Persian shield as the center of a large pot or planter. The dark purple leaves make a great contrast to silver-leaved plants such as Artemisia and dusty miller. They are an amazing accent for pink and white plants, and they are a bold color companion to orange or yellow plants.

Persian shield likes partially sunny locations and has excellent heat and drought tolerance. It sports pale violet, tubular flowers that are less showy than its foliage. Make sure to pinch it back often as it grows rapidly in warm temperatures.

The purple foliage of Persian shield is a happy mate to the red begonias in this shady bed planting in the Harry P. Leu Botanical Garden in Orlando, Florida. You can also use this combination in planters; place the Persian shield in the center of the pot.

Left: *Persian shield contrasts beautifully with yellow/green leaves of 'Illusion Emerald Lace' sweet potato vine (Ipomoea batatas) in a large pot.*

Right: *A stunning combo of iridescent purple leaves of Persian shield and the hanging pink flowers of showy Medinilla (Medinilla magnifica).*

112. LIFTING THE CANOPY

Do you have deep pockets of shade in your yard? Shadows cast by dense, leafy trees can make a space appear smaller than it actually is. You can make your outdoor area feel more spacious by removing the lower limbs of shade trees so that more air and light is allowed to filter in through the leaves. This time-honored pruning practice is called lifting the canopy.

The term *canopy* refers to a tree's branches that spread out over an area. The shade cast by a tree with a high canopy is lighter than normal, making the area more hospitable to the lawn or shade-loving plants beneath it. This is the dappled shade we all prefer. Thomas Jefferson extolled the virtues of lifting a canopy when he wrote:

> Let your ground be covered with trees of the loftiest stature. Trim up
> their bodies as high as the constitution & form of the tree will bear,
> but so as that their tops shall still unite & yield dense shade. A wood,
> so open below, will nearly have the appearance of open grounds.

Left: *Wide-spreading branches of the short-trunked naked coral tree (*Erythrina coralloides*) can be pruned in winter to allow more light to the ground.*

Facing page: *Taking off lower limbs of a tall shade tree like this pin oak results in a stately, vertical trunk leading to a high crown.*

113. TALL VERBENA—AN AIRY NONSTOP BLOOMER

If you want a sun-loving, summertime eye catcher, this is the flower for you. Tall verbena (*Verbena bonariensis*) is a graceful, deer-resistant flowering plant that sports lavender clusters of flowers atop wiry stems. It is a warm climate perennial (hardy in USDA Zones 7–11) that will grow to 6 feet tall in warm regions and 3 feet in the north. Grown as an annual in cooler zones, it is a nonstop bloomer from midsummer to frost. Plant it in a large group in a sunny location and watch the flowers wave in the breeze.

Tall verbena tolerates hot, dry, and sunny conditions and is a first-rate cut flower. Better than that, verbenas are a rich source of nectar for honeybees and butterflies. Protect it from strong winds and watch the pollinators gather round.

For a shorter variety, try 'Meteor Shower,' or 'Lollipop,' which grows to 2 feet tall. Their denser growth habit works well in containers and when massed in the garden. 'Meteor Shower' sets little seed, and so it does spread in the garden as most verbenas of this type do.

Left: *Tall verbena towers gracefully above other plants. It self-seeds aggressively and may volunteer itself around your garden.*

Below: *The profusely blooming tall verbena is both attractive and useful! It grows fast and attracts hummingbirds and butterflies to your garden. Looks great planted against a wall or fence.*

Here are some examples of fine-textured plants. Top left: 'Morning Light' Miscanthus. Top right: 'Dragon's Eye' Pine. Bottom left: the delicate Mexican feather grass. Bottom right: the moisture-loving Umbrella sedge.

114. FINE TEXTURES FOR FINE GARDENS

The soft, airy look of fine-textured grasses or the feathery foliage of threadleaf evergreens adds an ethereal look to a landscape. Fine-textured plants have slender, narrow leaves that form a great contrast to larger-leaved, more showy plants in the garden. They also act as a "harmonizer," blending various textured plants together. They are a great asset in planting design.

Soft, fine-leaved plants really come into their own when massed in large groups. There is nothing more striking than a tree underplanted with fine-leaved blue fescue (*Festuca ovina glauca*) or Mexican feather grass (*Nassella tenuissima*) in a grand swath. And a large mass of slender grasses such as purple love grass (*Eragrostis spectabilis*) or little bluestem (*Schizachyrium scoparium*) is especially eye-catching.

Fine-textured plants can actually make a small space appear larger because they tend to recede from view and let the bolder plants take center stage. The annual flower Euphorbia 'Diamond Frost,' is a good example of this. Other common fine-textured plants include lavender, maidenhair fern, bronze fennel, bleeding heart, and spirea. If you have a small space, make sure to add fine-leaved plants, as they will add some light and luster to your garden.

The wispy blades of 'Elijah Blue' Blue Fescue accentuates the flowers of Sedum 'Vera Jameson' beautifully.

115. THE SUNFLOWER—THE FOURTH SISTER

Native Americans are known for their traditional "Three Sisters" vegetable garden. They plant corn, beans, and squash together to benefit and protect each other. The system is ingenious and makes a lot of sense. Corn uses the nutrition supplied by the nitrogen-fixing roots of the beans. Beans need the support of corn as a place to climb. And the spreading squash plant, with its large prickly leaves, keeps weeds down, shades the soil, and deters four-legged raiders of corn. A very smart way to grow these crops.

But a fourth sister, the sunflower, can join the family in this garden. Sunflowers can be planted on the north side of a vegetable garden to keep the birds from devouring the corn. Why would they be placed on the north side? True sunflowers look to the sun and their faces follow it across the sky during the day. This heliotropic habit stops, however, when the sunflower is full of its delectable seeds. Then it stays facing the east. When sunflowers are planted to the north of the garden patch, they do not block the sun and birds see them in the morning when the light is upon them. Birds then dine on sunflower seeds rather than corn kernels. So everyone is happy when the fourth sister is planted in the vegetable garden!

Sunflowers always make us smile.

Sunflowers bloom happily in a vegetable garden in Lyle, Washington.

Left: *Sitting out in the sun can have a therapeutic effect. This is at the public garden in Rancho Mirage, California, called Sunnylands. A fitting name for sunlight therapy.*

Below: *Long shadows in the afternoon tell us that the day is coming to a close. When we see this, we instinctively start to get ready for the end of day.*

116. SUNLIGHT THERAPY

The soothing benefits of natural light can be enjoyed fully in a garden. The ancient Egyptian, Greek, and Roman societies all had healing sun temples because they knew that sunlight enhances mental equilibrium. Today, we know that access to sunlight can naturally increase production of vitamin D and help balance a person's circadian rhythms. Our bodies follow the sun and its cues. In fact, one hospital study found that patients in high sunlight rooms had less perceived stress, utilized fewer analgesic medications, and had reduced perception of pain. So why not place a chair in a favorite sunlit corner of your garden and enjoy the therapeutic effect?

You can create a "sun salutation garden" in an east-facing space for morning yoga or reveries. This sweet spot will allow you to enjoy the gentle morning rays. Similarly, you can lay out a walk that leads to the light. We all instinctively move forward on a path or corridor when light is ahead of us.

Sunlight also lets us know when it is time to relax. When we see the long outdoor shadows of late afternoon we sense that the close of day is at hand. When this happens, we instinctively start to slow down. Sunlight leads the way.

117. MIX AND MATCH SEDUM

Sedums are small, succulent plants that will grow in the tightest of spots. You can tuck these fleshy-leaved plants between paving stones, within garden walls, or in any sunny crevice. The versatility of these unfussy plants is a gardener's dream. Sedums make a great groundcover and can be mixed together to create a wondrous tapestry of differing colors and textures.

If you have a sunny spot and well-drained soil, you can expect a solid performance from sedums. Try growing taller growing sedums mixed with lower growing ones. A stunning combo is the dark purple foliage and pink flower clusters of the 14-inch-tall Sedum 'Purple Emperor' (USDA Zones 3–7) mixed with Lidakense sedum (*Sedum cauticolum* 'Lidakense') (USDA Zones 5–9), which grows 6 inches tall, has tiny silvery-blue foliage tinged with purple on its edges, and in late summer, features bright pink flowers. You can mix low-growing sedums together in a pot, on a rocky hillside, or in a sunny "hellstrip," that narrow bit of earth sandwiched between the street and the sidewalk. Easy-to-grow sedums always steal the show.

Top: *Snow in summer* (Cerastium tomentosum) *grows in and around yellow sedum Angelina' and purple-toned 'Sedum Lidakense'. It creates a treat for the eye.*

Bottom: Sedum cauticola *with the tiny blue/gray leaves blend with the glossy-green, fleshy, spoon-shaped leaves and yellow flowers of* Sedum kamtschaticum. *Yucca filamentosa 'Color Guard' is in the background.*

This grassed mound is in Innisfree, a wonderful landscape that is open to the public in Millbrook, New York.

118. PLAYFUL MOUNDS

Landforms can be so useful. A low mound covered in turfgrass in a landscape invites play and lounging. It makes a garden more interesting and can be used to direct drainage, block winds, and screen undesirable views.

It is best if a mound appears as a natural landform, so when you pile the soil, form an oval or free-form shape. In addition, a turf mound should be low and wide—a manageable height is about 18 to 24 inches high. The width should be at least 4 to 6 times as wide as the height. For example, if you have a 24-inch-high mound it should be at least 8 to 12 feet wide. This creates a gentle slope that fits into the surrounding area. Grassed mounds need to be less steep so that they can be mowed safely, but a mound can be steeper if you want to plant shrubs or trees on it.

This semicircular grassed mound is located on the grounds of American designer Jack Lenor Larsen's LongHouse Reserve in Easthampton, New York. This relatively high mound invites people of all ages to stop and spend some time here.

119. IN PRAISE OF COLEUS

Which foliage plant thrives in sun to part shade, is fast growing, and adds a colorful punch to planters and garden beds? The answer is the versatile coleus (*Plectranthus scutellarioides* cvs.), the tender tropical plant known for its vividly colored foliage. Its leaves can be red, burgundy, pink, green, yellow, white, and blends of these colors. Coleus comes in a range of sizes and growth habits. It does not need special care. What's not to love?

Coleus can be grown as an outdoor annual after danger of frost has passed. Buy small plants in spring, pinch them to promote bushy growth, and plant outside after night temperatures remain above 50°F. Make sure to give them adequate spacing. In midsummer, trim back the stems and leaves by about a third to promote stronger growth. By the way, coleus is one of the easiest plants to propagate. In fact, the plants will root in a glass of water.

The colorful leaves of the many varieties of coleus is a summertime dazzler. I plant coleus whenever I can—I mix it with evergreen shrubs, flowers, grasses, and in large pots outdoors. Its vibrant foliage shines in partial shade. There are sun-tolerant varieties as well. It is a praise-worthy plant indeed.

Got a shady spot? Here a group of planters filled with Coleus, Helichrysum 'Limelight,' and two colors of sweet potato vine (Ipomoea) create a foliar tapestry. That is 'Strawberry Drop' coleus in the planter on the right and 'Inky Fingers' coleus in the rear.

Left: *The bright limey yellow zing of 'Wasabi' coleus works well in both sun or shade. Here it is planted beneath a red-berried doublefile viburnum* (Viburnum plicatum tomentosum *'Mariesii').*

Right: *'Chocolate Covered Cherries' coleus has leaves with a rose center surrounded by mahogany and edged with a thin green margin. Looks great with asparagus fern as shown here.*

Above: *Did you know that the best time to turn over garden soil is during the last quarter of the moon (decreasing moon phase) because that's when the water table has dropped to its lowest point? The soil is not as wet and therefore you exert less effort and save your back!*

Left: *Just after the first crescent of the waxing moon there is a surge of energy through the plants and the sap begins to rise through the stems. Plant roses at this time, in the first or second quarter of the waxing (or increasing) moon.*

120. PLANTING BY THE MOON

The tradition of planting by the moon's phases has been around as long as humans have been growing food. We now understand that planting in tune with the moon's phases is a way to work with nature and her processes for our benefit. Wise gardeners use this method of planting and harvesting vegetables and fruit for good reason—it works!

You may know that the gravitational pull of a full moon causes the tides to be higher. Conversely, when the moon wanes, or becomes smaller, the water stays closer to the earth. The gravitational pull of the moon affects water in soil and plants too. When the moon is becoming full, or waxing, it pulls water upward in the soil and stimulates seeds to absorb more water and to grow faster. This is the time to plant aboveground crops. When the moon is on the wane, water in plants goes down toward the roots. Root crops can best be planted when the moon is waning. It is a much more complex system than this, and for the best advice on lunar planting, refer to the *Farmers' Almanac,* where gardening by the moon has always been their philosophy. They produce a calendar that describes the best days for sowing, planting, weeding, and other garden chores, as determined by the phases of the moon.

121. ANCHORS IN THE LANDSCAPE

An "anchor" in a landscape is a large element, in height or volume, that dominates an area and draws people to it. Just as a large, recognizable store in a shopping center attracts shoppers and benefits the smaller stores, a large rock, tree, or a small structure can be the anchor that pulls visitors to a certain part of a garden. Their larger size in relation to the elements around them lends an air of importance, and they lure visitors down the garden path to get closer to them. Anchors become a destination in a landscape.

A strategically placed large tree or a grouping of smaller trees make an effective anchor in a relatively large outdoor area. This is because they add a sense of scale. A large area becomes less imposing with an anchor feature. Similarly, in a smaller garden, an anchor can be a large rock, large colorful planter, or weighty sculpture. Light it up to enhance its importance at night.

Top: *I planted a circular grouping of 'Akebono' Yoshino cherry trees (Prunus x yedodensis 'Akebono') to act as an anchor in this landscape. They are especially appealing when they all bloom in the spring!*

Bottom: *This imposing oak tree dominates the landscape. Its height and spreading limbs make it the natural anchor for this garden. Everything takes second place to this beautiful specimen.*

Above: *Underneath the lacy, chartreuse leaves, the dark purple canes of 'Tiger Eyes' golden sumac are barely visible. But after the leaves fall, these branches look striking, especially in a snowy winter landscape.*

Below: *'Tiger Eyes' golden sumac exuberantly complements dwarf Chinese astilbes (Astilbe chinensis pumila) and white lilies in a plant bed at the Berkshire Botanical Garden in Stockbridge, Massachusetts. You can keep it looking tidy by pruning in late winter/early spring.*

122. TIGER EYES® CUTLEAF STAGHORN SUMAC

Are you interested in an eye-catching, golden-leaved shrub that is at home in sun to part shade and is tolerant of a wide range of soils? Tiger Eyes® cutleaf staghorn sumac (*Rhus typhina* 'Bailtiger') is such a shrub. It is hardy in USDA Zones 4–8, grows about 6 feet tall and wide, and has deeply dissected, bright yellow leaves that are up to 18 inches long. The leaves contrast well with a variety of plants, especially flowers. Discovered in a Minnesota nursery in 1985 as a mutation of cutleaf staghorn sumac (*Rhus typhina* 'Laciniata'), Tiger Eyes® is a "nativar," which is a cultivar of a native species.

The amazing foliage of Tiger Eyes® sumac starts off in the spring as chartreuse green and then changes to lemon yellow during the summer. It is in the fall when this stunner takes center stage as its foliage ranges from yellow to fiery orange/red, making it a showy addition to the landscape. Use it as a specimen in a plant border or near the patio.

But beware—this is not a plant for small spaces because it spreads slowly by underground suckers. For this reason, it is an effective soil stabilizer when planted in a large mass on a slope. It is a useful plant for erosion control and looks beautiful as well.

The deeply dissected, chartreuse leaves of Tiger Eyes® sumac are delightful against the deep blue flowers of larkspur.

123. LOVE YOUR SLOPE

We often see a steep slope as a liability, but I suggest you turn that around and see that hillside as a great asset to your landscape. If the hill faces you, then you are in luck. There before you is a wonderful opportunity to paint a garden "mural" to be admired from your house or patio. If you build some steps up the hill, your eye will automatically be attracted to them. Also, a diverse planting on a hillside allows you to see all the plants fairly equally, on the same plane. In other words, on a slope, you can appreciate all the plants as they are—stacked up the hill.

A planting arrangement on a slope plays with our spatial understanding. The plants in the distance do not disappear or get smaller as they do in a normal perspective. James J. Gibson describes how our eyes interpret this visual cue in his book *The Perception of the Visual World*: "If one thing appears above another it is probably not suspended in the air but merely lying on the ground at a greater distance."

Left: *Stone walls of varying heights retain this slope. After we built the walls, we planted boxwood, flowering iris, climbing hydrangea, and lady's mantle (Alchemilla mollis) to be admired from both below and above.*

Right: *Hydrangeas on a slope are the stars of a summer day. The flowers are displayed fully on this steep hill and are stunning during the day and into the evening. The steps we installed in the distance also help to draw the eye.*

The shape of the 'Dragon's Eye' pine is loose and open so give it a lot of room to grow.

124. DRAGON'S EYE PINE

'Dragon's Eye' pine (*Pinus densiflora* 'Oculus Draconis') is a variegated cultivar of Japanese red pine that originated in Japan centuries ago. Its name refers to the broad, yellow band that marks each long needle. The new candles have a striped appearance that creates a vibrant display when viewed from a distance.

This unique, two-needled pine is quite a specimen tree. It has a broad, asymmetrical shape with a flat top. After 10 years of growth, it will measure about 10 feet tall, ultimately reaching 20 to 30 feet tall and 15 feet wide. You can prune it yearly during the dormant season to encourage bushier growth the following spring.

The best way to show off this wonderful green-and-yellow tree is to plant it in front of a backdrop of evergreens or next to a house. Its irregular shape and the fissured red/gray bark make a bold statement. I plant an evergreen groundcover of myrtle (*Vinca minor* "Bowles") beneath it. Dragon's Eye pine can tolerate partial shade conditions but is fine with full sun with irrigation and moist soil. It may suffer some leaf burn from winter sun and icy winds, so a protected site is best.

The soft green-and-white needles of 'Dragon's Eye' pine look shimmering from afar.

125. ANGELINA STONECROP—A GARDEN WORKHORSE

Sedums, also called stonecrops, are taking the plant world by storm and for good reason—these small but tough succulent plants are well suited to the garden but also to the harsh conditions of rock gardens, green walls, and green roofs. They can survive with very little water, and many varieties have numerous flowers that are quite eye-catching.

'Angelina' stonecrop (*Sedum rupestre* 'Angelina') is a terrific, low-growing evergreen groundcover with small, needlelike leaves. It grows in USDA Zones 3–11 and is perfect for sunny, dry areas. It is a quick spreader that emerges with chartreuse foliage that turns golden yellow. It lights up rocky crevices and the front of garden beds. In summer, it sports clusters of yellow, starry flowers.

'Angelina' stonecrop grows equally well in planters and hanging baskets where its bright yellow leaves will trail over the sides. It can be pruned back at any time. As a bonus, its succulent foliage turns rich shades of orange and red in cooler weather.

Top, left: *'Angelina' sedum makes a great facer plant, in front of taller plants like the white daffodils shown here.*

Top, right: *Yellow Sedum 'Angelina' contrasts with the maroon leaves of Palace Purple coral bells peeking through at the Coastal Maine Botanical Gardens. This sedum spreads to cover the ground in a yellow mass.*

Bottom: *'Angelina' sedum can get a foothold in the smallest of cracks and then spreads fairly rapidly. Here it grows over a rock outcrop. Cooler weather causes it to turn a deep orange, creating a captivating ombre effect.*

Left: *The soil is very important for a vegetable garden bed. Notice how we "crowned" the soil, made it higher, in the center of the bed. This helps rainwater to run off to both sides.*

Below: *The soil supports the health of the plants. Nowhere is this more true than in a vegetable garden. Here the soil is raised above the mulched path.*

126. IT'S ALL ABOUT THE SOIL

Put simply, soil is not dirt. Soil is alive, filled with a vast assortment of organisms that breathe life into the land. Although we pay little attention to this microscopic world, mycologist Paul Stamets tells us that there are more species of fungi, bacteria, and protozoa in a single scoop of soil than there are plants and vertebrate animals in all of North America!

A garden is a reflection of the quality of its soil. Gardens filled with beautiful soil have a vitality about them that we can almost feel. But many properties today do not have healthy soil. The topsoil may have been skimmed off by the builder, or the original soil may be too heavy, rocky, or sandy. The most important aspect of a great garden is to have plant beds filled with healthy soil.

There are several ways to enrich your soil. Some people add amendments to the surface of the soil and let the microbes, earthworms, and other forms of soil life slowly incorporate it into the topsoil. This takes time. Another way is to turn over the soil to a depth of a foot or more, breaking up any clods. After turning, you can incorporate a variety of amendments depending on the needs of your soil. These amendments include topsoil, peat moss, compost, good-quality leaf mold, bagged manure, bone meal, worm castings, lime, and more. The quantities depend on the soil and its needs.

Kids need to touch the soil. Studies say it helps build up immunity.

127. VERSATILE ORNAMENTAL ONIONS

Ornamental onions, also known as ornamental alliums, are planted for their showy round heads of clustered starry flowers that top a clump of grasslike leaves. This hardy perennial, originally from Central Asia, comes in a range of sizes, shapes, bloom times, and shades (blue, purple, white, and yellow). The varieties vary in height from 3 inches to 4 to 6 feet tall. They come back every year and multiply naturally. Deer, rabbits, and most rodents don't bother them. How great is that?

These wonderful spherical flowers are undemanding. They like well-drained soil and full sun, and have no serious diseases or insect pests. Best of all, pollinators such as bees and butterflies flock to them! The pom-pom shape provides great contrast to the other flowers. Plant them with Russian sage, perennial blue salvia, and ageratum for a deer-resistant blue/purple garden!

Most alliums should be planted in the fall for a spring display, but a few, like 'Summer Beauty,' (*Allium tanguticum* 'Summer Beauty'), are planted in spring for summer blooms. One late summer blooming variety, Allium 'Millenium,' was named the Perennial Plant of the Year for 2018 by the Perennial Plant Association. It has masses of rose-purple blooms, 10 to 15 inches high, that last four weeks. 'Millenium' is heat tolerant and hardy from USDA Zone 4–9.

Plant Allium 'Summer Beauty' bulbs in spring for midsummer blooms of 2-inch lavender-pink flowers. Flowers are approximately 18 inches tall. Here 'Summer Beauty' is combined with the deer-resistant annual Salvia 'Victoria Blue.'

Left: *Nodding Onion (Allium cernuum) is a native plant that grows 12 to 18 inches tall. It has narrow, grasslike leaves topped with clusters of small bell-shaped lilac/ pink flowers that appear to "nod" sharply downward. Blooms in summer. Here it thrives on a sunny hillside at the Center for Sustainable Landscapes in Pittsburgh, Pennsylvania.*

Below: *The spheres of the popular 'Purple Sensation' allium are even more magical when paired with the white 'Mount Everest' allium. They bloom at the same time in late spring and grow to a similar 30-inch height. Plant in fall.*

Above, left: *The native river birch (Betula nigra) displays satiny, silver bark that peels to reveal a cinnamon-brown trunk beneath. It is a graceful, multi-trunked tree that can reach 80 feet in height.*

Above, right: *Lacebark pine (Pinus bungeana) is known for its distinctive flaking bark in tones of dark gray, tan, and reddish-brown.*

Left: *The 'Heritage' river birch (Betula nigra 'Cully') has beige and creamy white bark that naturally peels away from the trunk. It is quite dramatic in a garden. The tree grows to over 40 feet tall.*

128. GO FOR THE BARK

One way to add punch to a garden, especially if it is a stark, contemporary one, is to plant trees with unique bark patterns. This includes textured, mottled, or peeling bark. Bark used in this way provides a subtle yet artful touch that enhances any landscape. It also extends the seasonal interest of the garden well into the winter months, when most gardens have little to offer.

There are many trees that have unusual bark. These include birch trees, crepe myrtles, stewartia, Kousa dogwoods, eucalyptus trees, and lacebark pines. These trees are strong accents in the landscape, but it is their compelling bark that makes them even more special. Crepe myrtle trees have peeling strips of bark that reveal a smooth inner bark with colors that flow together like a paint-by-number painting. Japanese stewartia (*Stewartia pseudocamellia*) has bark that flakes off, revealing a striking mosaic of green, gray, reddish-brown, and beige. And 'Heritage' river birch (*Betula nigra* 'Cully'), a rapid growing, multibranched tree, is prized for its highly textural, colorful, peeling bark. It is a visual treat and is a candidate for uplighting at night.

It is simple: Go for the bark.

129. THE DELICATE BEAUTY OF THE LACELEAF JAPANESE MAPLE

The laceleaf Japanese maple (*Acer palmatum* var. *dissectum*) and its cultivars are undeniably beautiful. Their wide-spreading, low-branching shape features deep-cut leaves that form a delicate weeping effect. The leaves can be green, red, yellow, or a combination of these, depending on variety. They are as attractive in winter as in summer due to the sculptural framework of their graceful limbs and delicate twigs.

These slow-growing trees prefer part shade and moist, well-drained soil in a sheltered location. They are suited to USDA Zones 5–8, more or less.

The lacy leaves and weeping habit of these ethereal Japanese maples unify a garden by striking a visual balance between taller trees and shorter shrubs. They can be planted in the ground or in a container (in warmer areas). Because their roots are not aggressive they can be planted near rock outcrops or buildings. In time, they attain quite a stately character. They are always the centerpiece of a garden.

A popular form of this tree is the green laceleaf Japanese maple (*Acer palmatum* var. *dissectum* 'Viridis'). It has deeply cut leaves and grows to 5 to 10 feet tall. It flourishes in shade and has a beautiful yellow/orange fall color. Another popular cultivar is 'Crimson Queen' (*Acer palmatum* var. *dissectum* 'Crimson Queen'). This stunner has weeping branches of beautiful, deep red/purple foliage. In autumn, the finely cut leaves turn bright crimson.

Above: *The fluid shape of this green-leaved Japanese maple makes a shady corner come to life. Laceleaf Japanese maples love partial shade in the afternoon but some cultivars do well in direct sun provided they receive adequate water.*

Left: *The color of the red-leaved Japanese laceleaf maples become more vivid in the cooler weather of autumn. The combination of shape and fall color is memorable.*

Left: *Pastel-pink Flamingo Feather celosia is easy to grow—sow seeds directly outside in late spring. This sun-lover starts blooming in summer and lasts until frost.*

Below: *Celosia 'Caracas' is a show-stopper in the garden. It grows to 2 to 3 feet tall and sports dark magenta plume flowers that are light and airy. Pinch off the first blooms of the season to encourage bushy plants with more blooms.*

130. FEATHERY CELOSIA

I love feathery celosia! Known as wheat straw celosia (*Celosia argentea* 'Spicata'), this is a popular annual flower (USDA Zones 10–12) because it is so easy to grow. The botanical name, celosia, translates to "burning," which describes its upright plumes that resemble licks of flames. There are several varieties of sun-loving celosia, but I particularly like the wheat variety for its colorful, narrow blooms so reminiscent of seed heads of wheat. They are a hit with kids because the flowers are fun to touch.

The flowers of wheat celosia come in a range of colors and grow between 1 and 5 feet, depending on the specific variety. A classic is the 4-foot-high "Flamingo Feather." It has long stems of bicolored rose and deep pink flower spikes that fade from pink to white for an eye-catching effect. All the tall celosia varieties are perfect for a cutting garden because they are excellent as a dried flower.

My particular favorite is Celosia Intenz (*Celosia argentea spicata* 'Intenz'). It has bright fuchsia upright candles of flowers covering the plant, grows no higher than 12 to 16 inches tall, and blooms all season. Its color and shape spice up the flowerbed like nothing else can!

Celosia argentea 'Intenz'™ has bold and bright fuchsia/purple spiky flowers over purple-flushed foliage. 'Intenz' grows 18 inches tall and 12 inches wide. As it matures the lower part fades to white for a great effect.

131. A SHAPE, A VOLUME, AN ARABESQUE

*A garden is a complex of aesthetic and plastic intentions; and the
plant is, to a landscape artist, not only a plant—rare, unusual,
ordinary or doomed to disappearance—but it is also a color, a
shape, a volume or an arabesque in itself.*
—Roberto Burle Marx

It is not often that plants are referred to as an arabesque, which means a decorative line or motif. But it makes sense that a master twentieth-century landscape artist from Brazil, Roberto Burle Marx (1909–1994), saw plants in this way. He loved the native plants of Brazil and cherished their tropical shapes and textures. He discovered them not in Brazil but while working in Germany at an early age. He realized how beautiful they were, and so he synthesized art and horticulture. He treated tropical plants as artful elements and planted them in places such as the Botanical Garden of São Paulo.

Burle Marx's modern landscapes stand the test of time. He counsels us to view plants as part of a larger design palette, appreciating their form, line, or color; and to envision what they might add to the overall look and ecology of a garden.

Top, left: *Strong, sculptural leaves make a statement in a landscape. Here the pointed leaves of the variegated dracaena (Dracaena deremensis 'White Stripe') combine shape and a distinctive white edge to stand out against a tawny-colored wall.*

Top, right: *The yellow-and-green-striped, bold foliage of 'Tropicanna Gold' canna lilies steal the show. It contrasts nicely with the white flowers of the PG Hydrangea in the summer.*

Bottom: *The huge leaves of water-loving, freely spreading Butterbur (Petasites japonicus) are best grown on the shoreline of a natural pond or on the stream banks.*

132. A SPARKLING GROUNDCOVER—
'BEACON SILVER' DEAD NETTLE

'Beacon Silver' Dead Nettle (*Lamium maculatum* 'Beacon Silver') is a groundcover for part-shade conditions in USDA Zones 2–9. Its unique silvery foliage with a narrow green margin glows in the dimness. It is a fast grower to 8 inches tall and 20 inches wide, and its stems will root into the ground where they touch. Its other bonus is the clusters of bright purple flowers that adorn the plant from spring through early fall.

Once established, it tolerates dry shade fairly well. Lamium 'Beacon Silver' is a good companion with other shade lovers such as ferns, bleeding heart, hellebores, and coralbells. It can suffer dieback in summer but may rejuvenate in the coolness of autumn.

Use the low-growing 'Beacon Silver' dead nettle to edge a shady plant bed, or use it in a large mass beneath trees in a woodland garden. You might grow several varieties of Lamium together, such as 'Beacon Silver,' 'Pink Pewter,' 'White Nancy,' and 'Purple Dragon,' to create an interesting foliage tapestry.

'Beacon Silver' lamium is a great choice for a tough yet showy perennial groundcover in dry shade. Trim back in late winter.

133. LIGHT AS AIR—SPIDER FLOWER

In the heat of summer, the airy, drought-tolerant flowers of spider flower (*Cleome hassleriana*) take center stage. This deer-resistant perennial, which is grown as an annual in cooler climates, was considered an old-fashioned cottage garden flower that our grandmothers grew. It had spiny stems, foliage with a pungent aroma, and reseeded freely. That has changed due to the long-blooming and heat-tolerant varieties that are now available.

A native of South America, cleome thrives in ordinary soil and full sun, with little care. A tall heirloom variety, Cleome 'Rose Queen,' grows 4 feet tall and holds fragrant, 5- to 6-inch flower clusters at the top, making it a great plant for the back of a border. The deep rose buds open to lighter pink blossoms, and they have a whiskery look thanks to the stamens and pistil that protrude out several inches. Flowering all summer, the blooms attract butterflies and hummingbirds. Its long stems are perfect for bouquets.

The new compact hybrids are now taking the spotlight. The popular 'Senorita Rosalita' Cleome grows no higher than 24 to 36 inches tall and sports clusters of lavender/pink flowers all along the stem that consistently bloom from early summer through late fall. It is odorless with sterile flowers that don't produce seeds, and its stems have no thorns. It is best planted in large groups to make a swath of color, or it can be planted with petunias and cosmos for a sweet summer flower garden.

The blooms of 'Sparkler Blush' spider flower are light pink brushed with white. 'Sparkler' grows 36 to 48 inches tall. It looks great combined when a mix of 'Sparkler' white, lavender, and rose cleome are grown together.

134. 'MELLOW YELLOW' SPIREA

Spirea is considered a common shrub, but 'Mellow Yellow' spirea (*Spiraea thunbergii* 'Ogon') challenges that assumption. It is an early blooming, deciduous shrub that grows 3 to 5 feet tall and wide. Small, white blossoms appear in profusion in March through April before the leaves emerge, but it is the willowy, twiggy branches and leaves that make it notable. The wispy, fine-textured foliage starts out yellow, softens to a yellow-green in summer, and turns a lovely combination of reds, oranges, and yellows in the fall, making it a late-season star as well. Hardy to −30°F, it is easily pruned after flowering in spring.

'Mellow Yellow' spirea is a versatile, low-maintenance shrub that brightens up any plant bed. It likes sun, and it can be considered a filler as it fits in harmoniously with many plants. It grows fully down to the ground, and it makes a good front-of-border plant. Mellow Yellow is equally appealing with evergreens, flowers, or grasses. I have found that it partners beautifully with boxwood, azaleas, holly, or the maroon 'Diablo' Ninebark.

Top: *'Mellow Yellow' spirea blends well with large-leaved hosta and white-tinged dappled willow, as shown here. Its fibrous roots make it easy to grow close to other plants.*

Bottom: *The fine branches of 'Mellow Yellow' spirea are highlighted when grown in front of a dark, evergreen boxwood hedge. It prefers full sun but will tolerate afternoon shade.*

135. LIGULARIA 'BRITT-MARIE CRAWFORD'

Ligularia 'Britt-Marie Crawford' (*Ligularia dentata* 'Britt-Marie Crawford') is one of my favorite shade plants. Its large, glossy, maroon/black leaves with dark purple undersides form a bold mound in a garden. It adds a punch to any planting. It can grow in deep shade and is a great plant for the north side of a house, as long as it has a reliable source of moisture. It needs consistent watering to thrive. It spreads about 2 to 3 feet wide, 3 feet high, and it is suited for USDA Zones 4–9.

In late summer, 'Britt-Marie' sports large groups of daisylike, golden yellow-orange flowers. They grow atop purplish-black stems that rise above the broad, dark maroon foliage. What a visual treat!

This plant was discovered in Fife, Scotland, by Britt-Marie Crawford. After her death, her husband, James Crawford, honored his wife by naming the cultivar after her and introduced it to the trade.

You can grow Britt-Marie in beds, but it also works well as a centerpiece among other well-watered planters. It looks great paired with green and lime foliage plants. Try it with shade plants such as yellow creeping Jenny or 'Wasabi' coleus. Plant it in a large group in a moist or wet, shady area. It is particularly suited for locations along streams and beside ponds.

Above: *The golden yellow daisy like blooms appear in late summer, and the contrast with the chocolate/maroon leaves is outstanding.*

Top: *Here the dark maroon coloration of the ligularia leaves is quite evident. Plant them in a mass. Loves shade.*

Bottom: *The new growth of 'Britt-Marie Crawford' ligularia grows low to the ground. The broad, dark leaves grow to 6 inches across. Needs moisture. Great for a streamside garden.*

INDEX

Note: Page references in *italics* indicate photograph captions.

rosette plants, 219
rounded forms, 63
rounded steps, 102
Rowley, George, 26
"runway effect," 44
Ruskin, John, 222
Russian sage, 212

S
scented plants, 140
sedums, 248, 264
shade, types of, 30
shade trees, 239
shadows, 30
sheltered corner, 79
Sleepy Cat Farm (Greenwich, CT), *97*
slopes, 260
small space gardens, 156
smokebush, 220
'Snowflake' oakleaf hydrangea, 228
soil amendments, 267
soil quality, 205, 267
spent blossoms, 222
spherical elements, 43
spider flower, 279
spirea, 281
spirituality, 88
staddle stones, 39
Stamets, Paul, 267
Steinhardt, Michael, 188
Steinhardt Garden (Mount Kisco, NY), *109, 188, 222*
stepped hedges, 223
stepping stone path, 116
steps
    cedar log, 109
    in garden design, 92
    long, 95

outdoor, 112
outdoor step treads, 112
rounded, 102
Stonecrop (Cold Spring, NY), *72*
stonecrops, 264
stones. *See also* rock outcrops
    in Japanese gardens, 86
    and stone towers, 86
stone wall cap, 113
stone walls, 120
stroll gardens, 128
succulent plants, 219, 248, 264
sunflowers, 244
sunlight, effect on color, 172
sunlight, morning, 34
sunlight therapy, 247
sun salutation garden, 247

T
tall verbena, 240
"temperennials," 151
theme gardens, about, 124
3-4-5 triangle rule, 96
Tiger Eyes® cutleaf staghorn sumac, 259
treads, 112
trees
    blue evergreens, 195
    'Dragon's Eye' pine, 263
    laceleaf Japanese maple, 272
    shade, 239
    with unusual bark, 271
tropical splash gardens, 151
Tuin de Villa (Netherlands), *49, 200*

U
USDA Plant Hardiness Zones, 205

V
verbenas, 240
vining plants, 43, 156
visual illusions, 59
visualization, 17

W
walkways
    front, 110
    in garden design, 92
    paved, 92
    raised, 97
wall corners, softening, 43
walls, stone, 120
walls, stone caps for, 113
Warden, Phyllis, *159, 177, 210*
warm-season grasses, 215
water cascade, 75
Wave Hill (New York City), *49*
wheat straw celosia, 275
whimsical gardens, 136
white, shades of, 166, 176
White Garden (Lewisboro, NY), *166*
white-leaved plants, 192
Whyte, William H., 85
window boxes, 156
windows, framing views with, 48
"wish photos," 18
wooden bench, 51
woodland gardens, 51, 152, 208

Y
yellow colors, 161, 165
yellow-leaved plants, 183
yin and yang, 67